SCIENTISTS
AGAINST TIME

SCIENTISTS AGAINST TIME

The Role of Scientists in World War II

H. A. FEIVESON

Archway Publishing books may be ordered through booksellers or by contacting:

Archway Publishing
1663 Liberty Drive
Bloomington, IN 47403
www.archwaypublishing.com
1 (888) 242-5904

ISBN: 978-1-4808-5479-6 (sc)
ISBN: 978-1-4808-5478-9 (hc)
ISBN: 978-1-4808-5480-2 (e)

Library of Congress Control Number: 2017919302

Print information available on the last page.

Archway Publishing rev. date: 3/6/2018

To Carol, Dan and Stephanie, Peter, Laura
and Nupur, Julian, Levi, Jaya, and Ceci.

Contents

Preface

This book is aimed at readers, including older young adults who are interested both in World War II and in science and technology. Books and articles on the scientists in WWII generally are organized by scientific topic—radar, radio guidance, intelligence, rockets, and the like. (One exception is Paul Kennedy's *Engineers of Victory*.) Here the chapters are organized by the critical battles of the war, as is done in most histories of the war, which I believe is a more engaging way to capture the enthusiasm of readers, at the same time addressing many of the critical scientific and technical innovations that played a role in these battles.

The book grows out of a freshman seminar that I have given several times at Princeton, "Scientists against Time." These seminars are restricted to fifteen students, but the number of students putting down the seminar as their first choice each year was between thirty-five and fifty. Many of the freshmen who took the seminar had a keen interest and, in many cases, a good familiarity with the war, and also a great interest in science and technology. Several of the students were headed for a history or other bachelor of arts major, but most were aiming for a major in science or engineering. The syllabus for the seminars covered largely the topics included in this book, and the book also draws on presentations and papers done by the students on these topics.

Except for a few memoirs of scientists engaged in the war, I have relied mainly on secondary sources, including several excellent one-volume histories of the entire war or of key battles of the war. These are appended to each chapter.

Introduction

This book ventures to paint a picture of how scientists and other technical experts impacted the critical battles of WWII. The focus will be mostly on Allied scientists, notably the American and British, although with some excursions on what German scientists were doing—including the German development of the first long-range rocket, the V-2, and one of the first jets, the ME-262.

The battles covered include critically these:

The Battle of Britain—in which radar and the development of modern fighter aircraft played a crucial part.

The Battle of Intelligence—with focus on how the Allies broke the German Enigma code.

The Battle of the Atlantic against the German U-boats—where microwave radar, high-frequency direction finding, and operations research played critical roles.

The battle for command of the air—and the story of the long-range escort fighter, the Mustang P-51, the proximity fuse, and the V-2.

D-Day and the Allied invasion of Europe—and the importance of understanding weather and tides, and the role of artificial harbors, amphibious craft, deception, and radar.

The Manhattan Project—the development of the atomic bomb.

These battles and developments explain a lot of why and how the Allies won the war. They do, however, leave out two of the critical battlefronts of the war—the Eastern Front, where the Soviet victories at Stalingrad and Kursk, perhaps more than any other battles, reversed the tide of war in favor of the Allies, and the Pacific front, where the US island hopping in the central and southwest Pacific brought Japan to the brink of defeat even before the atomic bomb. They also leave out two industrial miracles of the war—how the Soviets were able to move much of their heavy industry to the Urals and beyond as Germany overran western Russia in 1941, and the stupendous arms output of the US economy as the United States converted its civilian economy with unprecedented speed. This latter may be best illustrated by the fact that the United States, which produced 3.5 million private autos in the last year of peace, 1941, produced virtually none during the war. By the end of the war, the United States was producing one B-24 bomber per hour! Scientists and engineers, of course, were critical in all these fields as in the ones covered in the book.

Although many of the scientific and technical innovations in the war are discussed in the following chapters, several important ones are only slightly touched upon or not discussed at all. These include many of the great medical advances made during the war, from penicillin to antimalarial drugs; various handheld weapons, such as the flamethrower and bazooka; impressive advances in ship designs, including modern aircraft carriers; and many other such developments.

Although these theaters of war and industrial developments are not covered in any detail, they are briefly discussed in chapter 1, which seeks to provide an overview of the war, providing a context for the more detailed chapters. But overall, this book will focus almost entirely on the Western Front in Europe.

If there is an overall theme to this book, it might be put this way. In early 1942, the fate of the Allies appeared dire. Germany had conquered all of Western Europe (other than Britain), and its armies were deep into Russia. Japan had overrun Manchuria, the Philippines, and the Dutch East Indies and was deep into China.

The Japanese were aiming at controlling half the world's population! They had struck a devastating blow to the United States at Pearl Harbor and appeared to have control of much of the Pacific Ocean. So in early 1942, Allied victory did not at all look inevitable, as sometimes we now take for granted. But the tide did turn, and in this, scientists played a critical role.

In discussing the role of scientists in the following, we should not forget the terrible human toll of the war. Latest estimates are twenty-one million uniformed military killed and forty million civilians. The latter number includes the victims of the Holocaust and other deliberate killings and starvation, the casualties of strategic bombing, and the wanton destruction of civilians as the German army swept east into the Soviet Union, and Japanese destruction in China.

As noted, the focus will be on Allied scientists. Although German scientists also were creative, overall, Germany was slow in realizing the role science could play. In 1940, the German general staff had decreed that no research or development should be pursued unless it promised military results within four months. The Germans did not have the desperation that the British had early in the war, and Germany never cultivated the easy working relationship between the military and scientists that happened in the West. The British and the Americans integrated scientists and military officers in assessing battlefield operations—the concept of operations research, which will be discussed later in the book— while the Germans never did. Not until late 1942 did the Germans make a desperate effort to spur scientific activity, and by then it was too late.

Timeline of WWII

Pacific Theater	Date	Year	Date	European Theater
• Japan invades Manchuria	September	1931		
		1932		
		1933		
		1934		
		1935	October	• Italy takes over Abyssinia
		1936	March	• Germany reoccupies the Rhineland
• Japan invades China	July	1937		
		1938	October	• Munich Crisis— Germany takes over the Sudetenland
		1939	March	• Germany marches into Prague and takes over all of Czechoslovakia
			September 1	• Germany invades Poland; start of WW2
		1940	April	• Germany overruns Norway and Denmark
			May–June	• Germany defeats France
			June	• Italy declares war on France
			July–September	• The Battle of Britain

Pacific Theater	Date	Year	Date	European Theater
			September September 17	• Italy invades Greece • Germany calls off invasion of Britain
• Pearl Harbor • Japan strikes Philippines, Thailand, Burma, Malaysia, Singapore, Dutch East Indies	December 7 December 1941–January 1942	1941	Spring–Summer Spring June 22 September 1941 December 1941–January 1942 December 1941–January 1942	• Germany attacks in North Africa (Rommel) • Germany takes over Greece, Serbia, and Crete • Barbarossa—Germany invades Soviet Union • Siege of Leningrad begins (ends January 1944) • Soviet counterattack in defense of Moscow • The Arcadia Conference in Washington, DC
• Battle of Midway • Battle of Guadalcanal begins (lasts until February 1943)	June 4–7 August–February 1943	1942	Spring August November	• Germany relaunches attack on Soviet Union, driving south toward Stalingrad • El Alamein—British Army stops German forces in North Africa • Torch—Allies invade Morocco and Algeria
• United States begins takeover of New Guinea (secured mid-1944)	June	1943	January January July–August July November	• German Third Army surrenders at Stalingrad • Casablanca Summit • Battle of Kursk • Allies invade Sicily • Tehran Summit

Pacific Theater	Date	Year	Date	European Theater
• United States invades Gilbert Island Chain—Tarawa	November			
• United States invades Marshall Island Chain—Kwajalein	January–February	1944		
• United States invades Marianna Islands Chain—Guam, Tinian	July–August		June 6	• D-Day—Allies land in Normandy
			June 22	• Bagration—Soviet massive attack on German forces
			August 25	• Liberation of Paris
• US troops land in Philippines	October			
• Battle of Leyte Gulf			December	• Battle of the Bulge
• United States invades Iwo Jima	February–March	1945	February	• Yalta Conference
			March 7	• Allies cross the bridge over the Rhine at Remagen
• United States invades Okinawa	April–June		April 12	• President Roosevelt dies
			April 30	• Hitler commits suicide
			May 8	• End of war in Europe
• Trinity—first test of a nuclear weapon at Alamogordo, New Mexico	July 16		July	• Potsdam (Berlin) Summit
• Hiroshima	August 6			
• Soviet Union invades Japan	August 8			
• Nagasaki	August 9			
• Japan surrenders; end of World War II	August 11			

CHAPTER 1

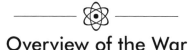

Overview of the War

Introduction
The March to War
German Victories in 1939 --1940
Battle of Britain
The Intelligence War
The Balkans and North Africa—Fall 1940–Spring 1941
The Eastern Front 1941–1942: Barbarossa—German Invasion of Soviet Union in 1941: Moscow and Leningrad
The United States Enters the War
    Pearl Harbor
    The End of Isolation
    Allied Grand Strategy
Battle of the Atlantic
The Mediterranean: 1941–1942
The Eastern Front 1942–1943: Stalingrad and Kursk
Allied Invasion of Sicily and Italy: 1943
Battle of the Pacific
    Battle of Midway
    The Island battles
    Tools of War
Medical Advances

Industrial Production
Strategic Bombing
D-Day and the Invasion of Europe
End of War in Europe
The Atomic Bomb and End of the War

Introduction

The following chapters of this book focus on six fields of conflict: the Battle of Britain, the Allied breaking of the German Enigma code, the Battle of the Atlantic, the battle for control of the air, D-Day and the Allied invasion of Europe, and the Manhattan Project to develop the atomic bomb. To provide some context for these battles and developments, this chapter provides a telescoped summary overview of the entire war, including of two critical theaters of the war not covered in the forthcoming chapters, the Eastern Front and the Pacific. Naturally, such an overview has to be highly selective in what it covers and sparing in specifics. The bibliography at end of the chapter includes several excellent one-volume histories of the war, which the reader may wish to consult.

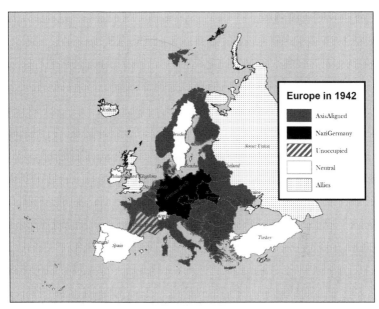

Fig. 1.1 Europe at Height of Nazi Domination 1942 (Laura Feiveson)

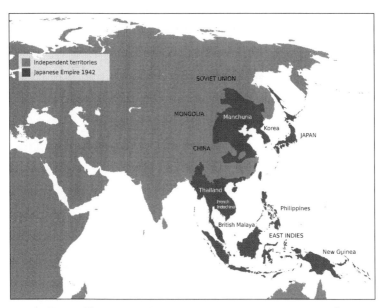

Fig. 1.2 The Japanese Empire 1942. Japan was aiming to control half the world's population! (T. Daniel Feiveson]

The March to War

How did the world go from WWI to WWII in just twenty years? For one factor, in purely strategic terms, Germany emerged from the Great War (WWI) stronger in some ways than it had entered the war. Its industrial base remained intact, and its industrial strength gave it the greatest economic potential in Europe. But German resentment smoldered. The Germans believed the Versailles peace agreement that ended the war to be unfair and unjust, and they longed to overthrow the treaty.[1]

Along with this pervading sense of resentment came economic hardships in the 1920s and then later in the Great Depression. And this potent combination led to the rise of Hitler and Nazism, and the capture of power by Hitler in 1933. Democracy also was lost in Italy and Japan during the 1920s when militaristic regimes assumed power. All three countries hungered to smash the international status quo—to gain control over other states and the resources of these states. Italy wanted to expand its colonial presence in a way it saw Great Britain and France having done. Japan, resource poor, also saw a parallel with Great Britain; if the British could have their colonial empire, why not Japan? Germany, however, after the rise of Hitler, had still greater ambitions.

The first jolt to the status quo was in 1931, when Japan invaded and occupied Manchuria, a rich province of China. And in 1937, Japan initiated a full war with China, moving deep into parts of China. Italy, for its part, invaded Abyssinia (Ethiopia) in 1935.

But the prime force for war, certainly in Europe, was unquestionably Hitler and the Nazis. From the beginning, the Nazis undertook to rearm and to erase the constraints of the Versailles agreement. From the beginning also, Hitler undertook to oppress the Jews and to promote a racist ideology. Inherent in the ideology was a belief in a German destiny to settle lands in the east,

Lebensraum (living space), taken from inferior Slavs in Russia. The looming tragedy is that, in the words of Antony Beevor,

> [A] critical mass of the population, desperate for order and respect, was eager to follow the most reckless criminal in history. Hitler managed to appeal to their worst instincts: resentment, intolerance, arrogance, and, most dangerous of all, a sense of racial superiority.[2]

German rearmament accelerated during the 1930s. Winston Churchill, a brilliant and resourceful politician and debater, and who for three decades had held prominent positions in the British government—home secretary, first lord of the admiralty, and chancellor of the exchequer among them—but out of power throughout the 1930s, warned with increasing urgency of the dangers posed by this rearmament, but few listened.

Indeed, German rearmament was countered by British and French appeasement, notably the policy of Neville Chamberlain, the British prime minister after 1937—that is, a policy of reacting only mildly to German provocations in hopes of appeasing Hitler. The provocations were not long in coming.

First, in March 1936, the Germans reoccupied the Rhineland, which had been under French occupation under the Versailles agreement. France and Great Britain simply accepted this. Starting in the summer of 1936, the Germans gave some, but limited, help to the fascists in the Spanish Civil War. In March 1938, Nazi Germany annexed Austria, an act supported by a majority of Austrians. This union with Austria (or Anschluss) removed Austria from the map of Europe for the next seven years! This had value for the Germans by allowing them to incorporate substantial foreign exchange assets owned by Austria.

In September and October 1938 came the Munich crisis. Hitler threatened to take over the German-populated Sudetenland region of Czechoslovakia on the grounds of uniting German speakers and sympathizers. Desperate to avoid war, Edouard Daladier, the French prime minister, and Chamberlain twice traveled to Germany to meet with Hitler, the second meeting in Munich ending by essentially giving Hitler the Sudetenland without a fight in return for a Hitler promise to have no further designs on the Czechs. That is, France and Great Britain refused to pledge to come to the defense of Czechoslovakia if it was attacked and persuaded the Czech government to accept the Nazi takeover. In the sad words of Chamberlain:

> How horrible, fantastic, incredible it is that we should be digging trenches and trying gas masks on here, because of a quarrel in a far-away country between people of whom we know nothing.[3]

Churchill, in the House of Commons on October 5, 1938, presciently gave voice to the likely consequences of the French and British appeasement:

> I do not grudge our loyal, brave people, who were ready to do their duty no matter what the cost, who never flinched under the strain of last week - I do not grudge them the natural, spontaneous outburst of joy and relief when they learned that the hard ordeal would no longer be required of them at the moment; but they should know the truth. They should know that there has been gross neglect and deficiency in our defences; they should know that we have sustained a defeat without a war, the consequences of which will travel far with us along our road; they should know that we have passed

an awful milestone in our history, when the whole equilibrium of Europe has been deranged, and that the terrible words have for the time being been pronounced against the Western democracies:

Thou art weighed in the balance and found wanting.

And do not suppose that this is the end. This is only the beginning of the reckoning. This is only the first sip, the first foretaste of a bitter cup which will be proffered to us year by year unless by a supreme recovery of moral health and martial vigor, we arise again and take our stand for freedom as in the olden time.[4]

In March 1939, despite Hitler's pledge during the Munich crisis, the German Army rolled into Prague, taking over the rest of Czechoslovakia. This at last shocked the French and British. It was clear that Poland would be the next target of Nazi aggression, and this led the French and British governments to issue an ultimatum that if Germany attacked Poland, that would be an act of war, committing the two countries to come to the defense of Poland.

After some sporadic and halfhearted attempts throughout the summer by the French and British to conclude an agreement with the Soviet Union to commit to defending Poland against a Nazi invasion got nowhere, on August 23, in a surprise that stunned the world, Germany and the Soviet Union signed a public nonaggression pact, along with secret protocols recognizing Soviet claims to part of Poland and other regions of East Europe.* Clearly now war was inevitable.

It started in fact one week later, on September 1, 1939, with

---

* This was the so-called Molotov-Ribbentrop pact—Molotov being foreign minister of the Soviet Union, and Ribbentrop the German foreign minister.

a massive German attack on Poland. As the German blitzkrieg (lightning war) drove deep into Poland, France and Great Britain initially dithered about honoring their commitment to Poland. In Britain, Chamberlain appeared to balk at declaring war, but a revolt in the House of Commons by members who felt that British honor was at stake forced his hand. In the midst of a torrential thunder and lightning storm, insurgent members of the House, in dramatic debate, pushed Chamberlain to declare war, which he finally did on September 3; the French followed soon afterward.

In the words of Williamson Murray:

> The rise of Nazi Germany represented a threat to the survival of Western civilization. Yet the shadow of World War I's slaughter exercised a powerful influence over statesmen guiding Western policy. ... The long road to 1 September 1939 was paved with good intentions, but in a world of Hitlers and Stalins, good intentions were not enough. Now only cold steel and the battlefield could defend the interests and hopes of Western nations.[5]

As noted above, Japan had taken over Manchuria in 1931 and invaded China in 1937. By 1941, Japan had over half a million troops in China and had control over large swathes of the country. But the war had settled into a kind of stalemate.

Japan's dream of empire was immense. Japan expected to extend military control over all Southeast Asia. And with control of the western Pacific and Southeast Asia, Japan would complete the subjugation of China. Japan's new order as envisioned by the men planning war in the fall of 1941 would include fully one half of the world's population![6] Japan came to believe that the key to achieving this new order was the destruction of the American fleet.

Many Japanese saw two basic causes of war: the unfair

distribution of territories and the unequal distribution of resources among nations.[7] Japan, like Britain, had limited natural resources, but Britain had an empire that appeared to secure its access to resources; Japan imagined it too should have an empire. In 1940, it termed this the Greater East Asia Co-Prosperity Sphere, meaning Japanese dominance in the entire East Asian region.[8]

Many in Japan realized war with the United States would be disastrous, but they could not see an alternative.[9] To reach an agreement with the United States and to keep getting oil from the United States, Japan would have to give up its China adventure, which already had cost it dearly, and its plans to expand to the south. Those changes in policy it could not accept.

The German victories in Europe seemed to Japanese leaders, especially in the military, a golden opportunity to make strategic gains while Britain and Russia were focused on Europe. On September 27, 1940, Japan concluded a pact with Germany and Italy. Though this pact did not commit Japan irrevocably to join war with the United States, if Germany and the United States were at war, it implied this. Germany was eager for a binding treaty to deter the United States from joining with Britain. The Tripartite Pact, signed in Berlin, pledged the signatories "to assist one another with all political, economic, and military means when one of the three Contracting Parties is attacked by a power at present not involved in the European war or in the Sino-Japanese conflict." It was aimed clearly at America.[10] The pact, of course, had the opposite impact on the United States than was intended, confirming to the United States that Japan was an aggressive power, like the Nazis, and had to be stopped.

This was the background that led Japan to take the momentous risk of attacking Pearl Harbor. Japan's chief objectives were to attack and occupy Malay and Singapore, Hong Kong, the Philippines, Thailand and southern Burma, and the Dutch East Indies. Such actions, especially in the Philippines, would be at risk unless Japan first destroyed much of US fleet.[11]

German Victories in 1939–1940

Despite valiant resistance by the Poles, German armor and aircraft overwhelmed the Polish defenses, and the Germans had achieved essentially complete victory by the end of October 1939. In the meantime, in a brutal campaign, the Soviet Union had taken over much of eastern Poland.

There now ensued a lull in the fighting, with little happening until the spring of 1940. There was not much France and Britain could do to help Poland, and Germany was (for the moment) content not to strike at other targets in Eastern Europe. France and Britain girded for war. Churchill, after the British declaration of war, had now entered the cabinet as first lord of the admiralty.

The lull in the war was broken decisively in April 1940 when German forces overran Norway and Denmark. Norway was, it turned out, a problematic victory for Germans: First, another revolt in the House of Commons ended the Chamberlain government and brought Churchill to power as prime minister. Also in the Norway campaign, Germany lost much of its surface fleet. And it tied up lots of German troops. As we will discuss in the chapter on D-Day, as late as June 1944, Germany still had 300,000 troops in Norway.[12]

However, these problems only became apparent later in the war. At the moment, Germany looked triumphant. And its greatest triumphs were yet to come. In May 1940, the Nazis struck again. In a lightning war spearheaded by tanks and tactical aircraft, they quickly overran the Netherlands and Belgium, and launched an attack against France. The critical operation in the attack on France was to send tanks and infantry through the heavily wooded Ardennes Forest, a maneuver that caught the French completely by surprise, routing the French army.

Some of the French leadership wanted to fight on—possibly moving the government to the French colony of Algeria. However, many, including Marshall Petain, eighty-four years old and a hero of World War I, who had been named premier a week earlier, feared internal upheaval more than he did the Germans. On June 22, he instructed the army to sign an armistice agreement with Germany—an agreement that took the French army and navy out of the war and gave Germany control over northern France, with the Petain government stationed in the town of Vichy in southern France nominally in control of southern France. The Nazi defeat of France in six weeks was stunning in its speed and completeness.

The Battle of Britain

Britain, which had sent an expeditionary force to France to meet the Nazi invasion, was now in great danger. Most of the expeditionary force appeared trapped in France. Hitler assumed Britain would now sue for peace. The critical war cabinet meetings were held on May 26–28 in which this possibility was discussed. The war cabinet consisted of Churchill, Chamberlain, Lord Halifax (the foreign secretary), and the leaders of the British Labor Party, Clement Atlee and Arthur Greenwood. However perilous the British position, the war cabinet was resolute—Britain would fight on. This determination was supported by a British Chiefs of Staff study, "British strategy in a certain eventuality," dated May 25. The study assumed the worst: France concluding an armistice agreement with Germany; French North Africa under German control; and the loss of most of the British expeditionary force. Even so, it concluded that Britain could survive—if Britain did not lose control of the air over Britain and the seas of the Atlantic and English Channel.[13]

Although as feared, France did fall, the British expeditionary force trapped in northern France and many French forces (340,000 Allied troops in total) miraculously escaped, though without their armor, in the Dunkirk evacuation that took place between May 26 and June 4. The dramatic evacuation was done by thousands of boats of all sizes taking troops from the Port of Dunkirk in France, ten kilometers from the Belgium border, in the face of attacks by the German air force.

Despite this rescue, however, Britain's position remained perilous. As the Chiefs of Staff study had argued, to survive, Britain would have to keep command of the air. From the German vantage point, for an invasion of Britain to be attempted would require the German air force, the Luftwaffe, to gain control over British skies. The Germans sought such control in the crucial air battles of July, August, and September—the so-called Battle of Britain. We discuss this battle in some detail in the following chapter. As discussed there, two technical developments played a central part in the battle—radar and the single-winged metal aircraft. Neither Britain nor Germany won the battle in the sense that the other side was defeated. But by not losing, Britain achieved its critical objective—not allowing Germany to gain control of the air over the English Channel, Germany's precondition for an invasion of the British Isles.

The Intelligence War

With radio communication (which could be listened to by enemies) becoming increasingly important to all belligerents, coding of messages was essential, and conversely, countries devoted great effort to breaking the codes of their adversaries. Two of the most successful such efforts were the Allies' breaking of the German Enigma cipher, and the United States' breaking of the Japanese diplomatic and naval ciphers. These developments are discussed in chapter 3, focusing largely on the breaking of Enigma, which to the end of the war the Germans thought to be impenetrable. The information gained by the Allies from reading the Enigma traffic was termed "Ultra" and played a role in all the European theaters of action mentioned below. The breaking of the Japanese naval code also was significant, perhaps most directly and dramatically in the battle of Midway, discussed later.

The Balkans and North Africa—Fall 1940–Spring 1941

With the German victory in France almost in hand, Benito Mussolini, leader of the Italian Fascist government, wanted to get in on the act, and on June 10, Italy declared war on France. In President Roosevelt's mordant words, "The hand that held the dagger has struck it into the back of its neighbor."[14]

And Mussolini was not done. He sent troops to North Africa to take on the British and, in September 1940, invaded Greece. Both were debacles for the Italians. The British routed the Italians in Libya, and the Greeks blunted the Italian invasion and drove the Italians back into Albania (a country that Italy had occupied in 1939).

The Italian defeats forced the Germans to take action, first in Greece and then in North Africa where Hitler sent General Ernest Rommel and the Africa Corps to battle the British. Germany soon overran Greek defenses, and in North Africa, Rommel gained some striking successes in the spring and summer of 1941.

Germany, also in the spring of 1941, invaded and occupied Serbia and Crete. On the eve of its invasion of Russia in June 1941, Germany, in addition to its occupation of Greece, Serbia, and Crete, had enlisted Romania, Hungary, and Bulgaria as Axis satellites.

The Eastern Front 1941–1942: *Barbarossa—Germany Attack on Russia, June 22, 1941, Moscow and Leningrad*

Hitler's decision to invade Russia was one of the most momentous of the war—and perhaps the most disastrous.

Hitler's wish all along was living space for Germany by taking over western Russia. Not only would decisive victory give Germany domain over the vast resources of western Russia, by starving the conquered inhabitants, it would provide living space for the

German race. Hitler believed that time was not on Germany's side: Russia was rearming, and he feared that the United States would join the war in a year or two. Invasion of Russia of course risked a two-front war, but Hitler believed Britain would be forced to sue for peace once Russia was defeated.

On the eve of the German invasion (termed Barbarossa), the Germans had mobilized two million men and had poised at the Russian border 3,600 tanks and 600,000 horses! Also 600,000 motor vehicles, 700,000 field guns and other artillery, and 2,700 aircraft. This was the largest invading force assembled in the whole of human history to this point.[15]

The Soviet Union was ill prepared to face the looming threat; and in this, Josef Stalin, chairman of the Soviet Politburo, was much to blame. In the years before, he had destroyed the officer corps of the army in a series of purges. "Of the 101 members of the supreme military leadership, 91 were arrested, and of these 80 shot."[16] In 1940 and the first six months of 1941, he had sent valuable resources, oil and machinery, to Germany in hopes of appeasing Hitler. Stalin knew Russia was unprepared and wanted to do nothing to provoke Germany.

Furthermore, in fear of giving up territory, he insisted that the Russian army station themselves at the western border rather than at more defensible positions in the interior. Above all, he had stubbornly ignored multiple warnings from the West and from his own intelligence services that the Germans were marshaling their forces for an invasion. For example, a Soviet agent in Rome on June 19 passed on information that Germany would attack sometime between June 20 and 25.[17] When the blow came, on June 22, 1941, surprise was complete. The scale of the catastrophe was unprecedented. German advances during the summer were staggering; Soviet losses were devastating—anywhere from five million to eight million Soviet citizens dead.[18]

By September, German forces had reached the outskirts of

Leningrad and placed a suffocating ring around the city. General Georgi Zhukov was sent by Stalin to save the city, and through brutal but effective methods, he did contrive to halt the German advance. According to Murray, Zhukov may have been the greatest operational commander of the war.[19] The siege of Leningrad, which lasted almost two and a half years,* caused over one million deaths—mostly of civilians—from bombing and artillery attacks, starvation, disease, and cold. But the city remained in Soviet hands.

In the invasion of Russia, "everywhere the Germans advanced, the tide of murder, violence, and destruction followed, on the Jews above all, but on the Soviet population in general."[20] Few German officers objected to the brutality of treatment, where prisoners and other Russians were left to starve. In this brutality, Hitler and the German generals were in accord. The Germans never sought to exploit the deep-seated hostility to Stalin's tyranny that much of the Russian population felt.[21] Over the course of the war, German forces took 5.7 million Soviet prisoners. Official German records showed that 3.3 million of them had perished by the time the war was over. The actual number was probably a good deal higher.[22]

Given the successes so far, in September, Hitler determined to attack Moscow. But the decision to go for Moscow in 1941 was not wise in light of the lateness of the season, the pervasive lack of supplies, and the serious losses that mechanized and motorized divisions had suffered since July. Still more critically, in the advance on Moscow, the Germans ran into the Russian winter. German preparations for winter remained almost nonexistent. Germany had not prepared for a long war or one over such great distances, where logistics became critical.

Zhukov rushed to Moscow to organize its defense. As

---

* The siege started on September 8, 1941, when the last road to the city was severed. Although the Soviets managed to open a narrow land corridor to the city on January 18, 1943, the siege was finally lifted on January 27, 1944, 872 days after it began.

German forces bogged down first in the muds of autumn and then in the fierce winter of 1941—reportedly the most severe winter since Napoleon's ill-fated invasion of Russia in 1812—Zhukov, in December 1941, organized a counterattack that halted the German advance just miles from Moscow and then drove the Germans back hundreds of miles. Fighting slid to a halt in March 1942 as the Germans solidified new battle lines.

The United States Enters the War

Pearl Harbor

In the early morning of December 7, 1941, Japanese planes launched an attack on Pearl Harbor, the US naval base in Hawaii. Toward Pearl Harbor the Japanese had sent six carriers, 423 planes, two battleships, three cruisers, three submarines, and nine destroyers. The carrier pilots were the elite of the Japanese navy. The attack took the United States completely by surprise. Out of a total of eight battleships anchored at harbor, two battleships were immediately sunk with great loss of lives. Six other battleships were badly damaged. Thus, the main surface battle fleet of the United States was devastated. The one saving grace for the United States—and a critical one as events later unfolded—was that no aircraft carriers were at the harbor. The United States was now at war.

Four days later, on December 11, Hitler declared war on the United States. During the fall of 1941, Hitler was cautious about provoking the United States, despite US anti-U-boat activities and pleas by the U-boat command pushing for attacks on American shipping. But Pearl Harbor brought the issue to a head. Although the Tripartite agreement with Japan (and Italy) committed Germany to war with the United States only explicitly if the United States attacked Japan, an informal agreement seemed to commit Germany even if Japan attacked the United States. In any event,

Hitler believed that the United States would inevitably enter the war against Germany in any case and that once it did, its impact on the war would not be felt for a year or more. The German navy strongly supported war against the United States. American shipping presented targets German submarines could attack. And the army could not have cared less. The declaration of war was one of the worst decisions Hitler made. By the action, he allowed Roosevelt to portray Germans and Japanese as a united enemy.

Along with the attack at Pearl Harbor, the Japanese struck elsewhere: the Philippines, Hong Kong, Thailand and southern Burma, Malaysia and the great British naval base at Singapore, the Dutch East Indies (Indonesia today), and several islands in the Pacific, including Guam and Wake Island. The Dutch East Indies was a critical Japanese object due to its oil fields vital to the Japanese war effort.

The End of Isolation

Pearl Harbor ended at one stroke a political struggle that had raged in the United States the previous two years between those who wanted to do all they could short of war to help the Allies (Great Britain, and including Russia after the German invasion in June 1941) and those wanting the country to keep to a strict neutrality.

During the 1930s, the combination of the Great Depression and the memory of tragic losses in World War I (over 50,000 US soldiers killed in the war) contributed to pushing American public opinion and policy toward isolationism. Isolationists advocated noninvolvement in European and Asian conflicts, which seemed far away and no apparent threat to the United States. Congress passed four neutrality acts between 1935 and 1939. These acts, which made no distinction between aggressors and victims, sought to ensure that the United States would not become entangled in foreign conflicts. They were largely repealed in 1941.

Although President Roosevelt early on grasped the dangers to the world (including the United States) if the Nazis came to dominate all of Europe, he realized that the country was not yet ready to join the British as a full-partner ally with a declaration of war against Germany. Nevertheless, there was strong pressure from inside the cabinet to intervene more forcefully in support of Great Britain.* Balancing these and competing pressures, Roosevelt gradually worked to help the Allies in all ways short of war. In this he was supported by prestigious citizen groups—notably the Committee to Defend America by Aiding the Allies and the Century Group.

Opposed to this policy were several influential senators** and various citizen groups, among them the America First group whose most prominent members included Charles Lindbergh and Col. Robert McCormick of the *Chicago Tribune*. Lindbergh, the popular and widely admired aviation pioneer—the first person to fly across the Atlantic—was the most visible of the isolationists. The angry fights between the interventionists and isolationists riveted the country for the two years, often dividing families. The sister and mother of Anne Morrow, Lindberg's wife, for example, were pro-intervention.[23]

In the country as a whole, in May 1940, only 35 percent favored aid to Britain and France at the risk of American involvement. But with the fall of France, isolationist feeling was weakening. There was now massive support for wholesale rearmament. And with increasing confidence that Britain could hold out against the Nazis, support for helping Britain began to rise. One dramatic moment that strengthened American determination to aid Britain was the

---

* These cabinet members included Secretary of War Henry Stimson, Secretary of the Navy Frank Knox, Secretary of the Treasury Henry Morgenthau, and Secretary of the Interior Harold Ickes.

** Including Burton Wheeler of Montana, Hiram Johnson of California, Gerald Nye of North Dakota, and William Borah of Idaho.

British scuttling of the French fleet anchored in Algeria on July 3, 1940, an action that underscored to Americans Britain's determination to fight on.

In September 1940, in a deal concluded by executive action, the United States agreed to transfer fifty destroyers to Britain in exchange for the British leasing bases in Bermuda, the Bahamas, Jamaica, Trinidad, and Newfoundland to the United States. The destroyer deal did not have much immediate impact, but it had tremendous symbolic significance. As was widely recognized, America had now effectively abandoned neutrality.

A still more decisive step toward intervention was taken by the Lend Lease agreement announced in December 1940 and passed by Congress in March 1941. Lend Lease was an ingenious stratagem dreamed up by Roosevelt, in which the United States would "lend" war material to Great Britain without demanding that Britain pay for the material. In a press conference on December 17, 1940, Roosevelt introduced the concept to the nation with a homey analogy: that when your neighbor's house is on fire, you lend him your hose, and when the fire is out, he will return it. Shortly after this press conference, Roosevelt made a fireside chat to the nation announcing that the United States must become "the great arsenal of democracy." By the fall of 1941, 70 percent of Americans were ready to help Britain even at the risk of American involvement in the war. The Destroyer deal and Lend Lease were factors perhaps that led to Hitler's decision to invade the Soviet Union before the United States could get into the war in a significant way.

By 1941, the United States was taking an increasing part in the war in other ways. In April 1941, President Roosevelt extended the Pan-American Security Zone east as far as Iceland. British forces occupied Iceland when Denmark fell to the Germans in 1940, and now US forces would relieve British troops on the island. American warships began escorting Allied convoys in the western Atlantic as far as Iceland and had several hostile encounters with U-boats. It was probably just a matter of time before such encounters escalated to all-out war. But Pearl Harbor ended all debate.

Allied Grand Strategy

The hallmarks of American and American-British grand strategy once America entered the war were simple and straightforward:

First of all, the Americans and the British committed to coalition warfare; to an unprecedented degree, the two countries evolved a joint high command, and in the field a high degree of cooperation. The commitment to coalition warfare was forged at the Arcadia Summit held in Washington from December 22, 1941 to January 14, 1942, where Churchill and Roosevelt and their aides established the combined chiefs of staff.

Secondly, despite some public pressure for the United States to focus on Japan after Pearl Harbor, the Americans, after they entered the war, affirmed a Germany first strategy.

Thirdly, America recommitted to mobilize its industrial resources to become "the arsenal of democracy."

Fourthly, the Americans and British committed to the extent possible to aid the Soviet Union in its climatic battle with the Germans.

Finally, from the beginning, the United States and Britain placed at their highest priority winning the Battle of the Atlantic (discussed below).

These goals were effectively renewed at the high-level Casablanca Conference in January 1943, attended by Churchill and Roosevelt. At this conference, the Americans and British for the first time announced their demand for unconditional surrender by Germany and Japan.

Battle of the Atlantic

The Battle of the Atlantic—the relentless, deadly fight between convoys, bringing vital resources from America to Britain and Russia, and German U-boats, which raged over the entire course of the war—is the subject of chapter 4.

In the early stages of the war, Ultra played a key role in locating U-boat wolf packs and diverting convoys away from them. But in much of 1942, the Allies lost the ability to decipher the German Naval Enigma, and convoy losses mounted. As late as March 1943, the U-boats, with minimum losses, sank over 600,000 tons of cargo, a devastating level.

In the next three months, however, there was a remarkable reversal of fortune. U-boats truly became "iron coffins"—any tour out to sea was likely to be a German submariner's last. Of approximately 40,000 submariners, 28,000 were killed. From the summer of 1943 to the end of the war, convoys plied the Atlantic almost unmolested.

One critical factor in the turnaround was the closing of the air gap in the North Atlantic. Until 1943, Allied aircraft from bases in Canada, Greenland, Iceland, and Britain were not able to reach a several-hundred-mile swathe in the Atlantic. But with the release of long-range bombers from strategic bombing roles in 1943 and the introduction of midsize aircraft carriers, this changed. And, as related in chapter 4, science and technology also played a crucial role in this turnaround—high-frequency direction finding, new weapons to supplement depth charges, operations research (developments explained in the chapter), and, perhaps most important of all, microwave radar, which allowed the detection of U-boats from escort vessels and patrol aircraft.

The Eastern Front 1942–1943: Stalingrad and Kursk

In the spring of 1942, after their winter setback, the Germans renewed their offensive, this time focusing on the south, driving for the Caucuses and Stalingrad, on the Volga. Again the initial German advances were dramatic, and by November they were on the outskirts of Stalingrad. The Russians fought desperately, suffering great casualties, and Stalingrad remained in Soviet hands. In the meantime, Zhukov was planning a counterattack on the highly stretched line of the Germans and their Romanian allies. The attack was launched in late November 1942, and the Third German Army pressing against Stalingrad was quickly encircled. Attempts to break through the encirclement failed, and in January, the army surrendered.

By spring 1943, the Germans had stabilized their defensive line and were plotting a counterattack at the so-called Kursk salient. The forces were assembled for what was to be the greatest land battle in history. It involved a total of four million troops, 69,000 artillery pieces, 13,000 tanks and self-propelled guns, and nearly 12,000 combat aircraft.[24] The Red Army outnumbered Germans in men and tanks, two or three to one.

The German attack was finally launched in July. But the Russians had prepared defense in great depth and blunted the German advance, and then in August launched their own counterattack. This counterattack routed the Germans. By the end of the summer, the Russian advance slowed, but from then on, the Germans were always on the defensive. The balance of forces on the Eastern Front had shifted and would never again be reversed.

How did the Soviets achieve so much, in first stopping the German blitzkrieg (lightning war featuring rapidly moving armored vehicles and aircraft supporting the ground operations) and then decisively forcing the Germans on the defensive? The most important reason was the tremendous tenacity and courage of the

Soviet defenders, fueled increasingly by a bitter hatred of the Nazi invaders—a hatred earned by the vicious German treatment of civilians in their path and of prisoners of war.

Certain technical developments, however, also played a part. For one, the T-34 tank, especially after late 1942, proved fast, mobile, and effective.[25] The Katyusha rocket, mounted on highly mobile trucks, also was used with devastating effect. In addition, to stop the German Panzers (tanks), the Soviets imaginatively deployed antitank missiles, mine fields, and ditches. The Soviets also proved adept at camouflage and other deception techniques to confuse the Germans where and when attacks were coming. In addition, as soon as the Kursk battle commenced, 100,000 guerillas began sabotage operations behind the German lines, destroying locomotives, railroad carriages, and bridges—plus providing intelligence.

At the same time, Soviet industry, much of it transferred dramatically from western Russia in the face of the German advance to the Urals and beyond, produced prodigiously, turning out artillery, tanks, and airplanes in great numbers. Overall, between July and December 1941, as the Germans were overrunning western Russia, the Russians transferred over 1,500 enterprises, mostly iron, steel, and engineering plants, to the Urals, Volga region, and Kazakhstan. In 1942, the Russian economy produced more weapons than the year before, and more than did Germany. Between 1942 and 1945, the Soviet Union produced half again as much as the Germans.[26]

The Mediterranean—1941–42

As earlier noted, with the Italians faltering in Libya at the end of 1940, the Germans intervened. In February 1941, they sent in the Africa Corps under the leadership of General Erwin Rommel. Rommel for over a year had several spectacular successes. By the summer of 1942, Rommel and the Africa Corps were moving into Egypt and threatened the Suez Canal.

By then, however, General Bernard Law Montgomery had taken over the British Eighth Army. Montgomery proved to be one of the great field commanders of the war. "He was not a nice person: dogged, conceited, vain, and completely sure of his own abilities, and incapable of understanding other human beings, he was also possessed of the attributes of a great general. Rigorous, enthusiastic, flexible, first rate trainer, understood the common soldier, understood the strengths and weaknesses of his forces and decided strategy accordingly."[27]

At the same time, Rommel was severely hampered by shortages of oil and material. The Allies, by virtue of reading German and Italian coded messages, located ships headed to supply Rommel and inflicted great damage.

In August 1942, at the Egyptian coastal town of El Alamein, the British Eighth Army halted the German advance. And with growing superiority in men, tanks, artillery, and aircraft, it began to take the offensive. Then, on November 8, an Anglo-American army landed in North Africa—Morocco and Algeria—under the command of Dwight Eisenhower. In the words of Williamson Murray, "Eisenhower had great gifts: enthusiastic and jovial, a will of iron, and extraordinary intelligence. Unlike many of the American and British high command, he was willing to subordinate his ego for the greater good – the ideal commander of the Allied coalition."[28]

With the Allies pressing from the west and the Eighth Army from the east, German and Italian forces collapsed. In April and May 1943, the Allies captured 275,000 German and Italian soldiers. North Africa and the Mediterranean were now firmly in Allied hands.

Allied Invasion of Sicily and Italy—1943

In July 1943, the Allies launched an amphibious landing on Sicily and soon took possession of the island. Although the invasion was not a full success in that it allowed most of the Germans to escape to the Italian mainland, it did lead to Mussolini's overthrow.

The success of the landing was helped by an audacious deception campaign that persuaded the Germans that the coming attack the Allies were clearly planning was not aimed at Sicily but rather the Balkans and Greece. This campaign of deception was highlighted by so-called Operation Mincemeat, in which a body purporting to be a British officer was washed up on the shore of Spain with plans for an attack on Greece chained to his wrist. This was the "man who never was."[29]

In September 1943, the Allies invaded southern Italy. By then the Italians had accepted the Allied armistice conditions, but this came too late—the Germans had taken over. The Allies liberated Rome on June 4, 1944, two days before D-Day. But the Italian campaign slogged on to the end of the war.

The Pacific War—1942–1945

As noted above, many Japanese strategists had deep qualms about engaging in a war with the United States. As matters turned out, these qualms were amply justified.

Battle of Midway[30]

After Pearl Harbor and its early 1942 conquests, Japan had several choices. It could seek to expand into the Indian Ocean, or to attack in the South Pacific as prelude to an invasion of Australia, or to resume a naval thrust across the central Pacific. It chose the last.

In light of this strategy, Japan sought to lure the US Navy into a great battle that would destroy the US naval forces in the Pacific. Its way of doing this was to launch an attack on the US naval base on Midway Island, a small atoll, six miles across, about 1,300 miles west of Hawaii. The Japanese reasoned that to protect the base, the United States would have to send its remaining fleet to defend (or retake) the island where it would be exposed to annihilation by a much stronger Japanese fleet. And indeed the force that Japan sent to Midway consisted of seven battle ships, twelve cruisers, forty-four destroyers, nineteen submarines, and four aircraft carriers hosting the elite of the Japanese air force. By contrast, the United States had sent into the battle only eight cruisers, three aircraft carriers, and twelve submarines.

But the United States had one great advantage. It had broken the Japanese naval code. This had revealed the Japanese intention to invade Midway, the character of the invasion fleet, and the time of the invasion. Armed with this information, the United States sent its carriers to the northeast of the island, waiting for the Japanese attack.

On June 1, the Japanese launched its air attacks on Midway, with partial success. The United States, warned of the coming attack, had sent most of its aircraft into the air safe from the Japanese bombers. As the Japanese readied themselves for a return attack to finish the job of destroying the Midway airfields, the United States had in the meantime discovered the location of the Japanese carriers and sent out waves of torpedo and dive-bombers. The torpedo bombers were largely shot out of the sky by the Japanese Zero fighters, and no Japanese carriers were hit. (Of forty-one torpedo planes launched from the carriers, only four made it back.)

But as the decks of the carriers were clogged with aircraft ready to take off, suddenly out of the clouds, the US dive-bombers struck, driving downwards at 250 miles per hour. In ten minutes, ten bombs destroyed three of the Japanese carriers—the bombs detonating the fuel stacked on the decks. Several hours later, US dive-bombers crippled the fourth Japanese carrier, and on the following day, it sunk. A Japanese counterstrike from that carrier before it was itself attacked badly damaged one of the US carriers, the *Yorktown*, and it too was eventually lost. Along with the loss of the carriers, the Japanese lost the cream of their air pilots—a devastating loss. After the war, the Japanese naval commanders all saw Midway as the decisive turning point of the war. In the two years after Midway, the Japanese built four new carriers, the United States ninety![31]

The Island Battles

After Midway, the United States was faced with the decision of how and where to attack the Japanese. In broad outline, it had three possible routes to pursue:

- Press attacks on the Asian mainland to approach Japan through China and Southeast Asia.
- Mount an island campaign northward from Australia, New Guinea, and the Philippines.
- Mount an island campaign through the central Pacific.

To some extent, the United States pursued all three avenues. It gave some attention to the China-Burma Theater, in various ways helping the Chinese in their battle with Japan. Although this theater of operation did not consume a large part of US resources, it did tie down a large number of Japanese troops.

For the New Guinea-Philippines route, the United States poured in men and material, under the overall leadership of General Douglas MacArthur. MacArthur led an advance along the New Guinea coast, hopping over and isolating several Japanese strong points. On October 20, 1944, with overwhelming naval and air power, the United States commenced the liberation of the Philippines by an amphibious landing on the eastern-most island of Leyte. The island of Luzon and it chief city, Manila, were not taken until February 1945, and in fact hostilities on small parts of the islands continued through the end of the war in August. Although the southern route to Japan at the end did not play a critical role in the defeat of Japan, it did tie down a great number of Japanese forces.

The critical route to Japan, however, was the island hopping in the central Pacific, where the United States moved increasingly closer to Japan, close enough to launch devastating bomber attacks.

The islands attacked and occupied included Tarawa in the Gilbert chain of islands, Kwajalein in the Marshall Island chain, Saipan, Guam and Tinian in the Marianas, Iwo Jima, and Okinawa, each island drawing the United States closer to the Japanese mainland. The Japanese, fighting almost literally to the last man, made the United States pay dearly for the island conquests. On Iwo Jima, the Japanese suffered nineteen thousand killed, with only two hundred taken prisoner; the United States suffered seven thousand killed and twenty thousand wounded. On Okinawa, over eighty thousand Japanese troops were killed, and again comparatively few surrendered; the United States lost fourteen thousand killed. In addition, tens of thousands of civilians were killed under the intense crossfire or, driven by the Japanese army, committed suicide.

The island conquests gave the Americans the airfields necessary for the bombing of Japan, and by 1945, the bombing raids were devastating the Japanese economy. The culmination of the bombing offensive was when a B-29 armed with an atomic bomb took off from Tinian toward Hiroshima on August 6, 1945. This and what led up to it are discussed in chapter 7.

Tools of war

Although the scientific and technical achievements in the Pacific theater are not discussed in detail in this book, they were substantial. They included the development of amphibious craft of many kinds; the Essex-class carriers, able to reach thirty-knot speeds with one hundred aircraft on board; and the Grumman F6F Hellcat fighters that could outclimb, outturn, and out-dive any Japanese craft. During the war, the Hellcats flew more than 66,000 sorties, almost all from decks of carriers, and destroyed 5,163 enemy aircraft, with a loss of 270!

The United States also deployed hundreds of modern submarines. The submarines devastated Japan's ability to import oil and other materials into Japan. Japan tankers delivered only one-tenth of the oil produced in 1944–1945. Of the 3.8 million tons of Japanese shipping of all classes sunk in 1944, US submarines destroyed 2.3 million tons.

The bombing of the Japanese mainland was carried out mainly by the B-29 Superfortress. The development of this aircraft required unparalleled advances. It was twice as heavy as the B-17, was pressurized to fly at over thirty thousand feet, and had a top speed of 350 mph, a range of over 3,700 miles, and a payload capacity of twenty thousand pounds. The development of the bomber involved vast resources. It has been estimated that the development cost 50 percent more than did the Manhattan Project.[32]

The critical role of the construction battalions or CBs (the SeaBees), under the direction of Admiral Ben Morell also deserves note. Over the course of the war, in the Pacific, the CBs built 111 airstrips, 441 piers, tanks for storage of 100 million gallons of gasoline, housing for 1.5 million men, and hospitals for seventy thousand patients. In Europe, as we discuss in chapter 5, the CBs built the Mulberry harbor for D-Day and rebuilt the ports of Cherbourg and Le Havre. They also dismantled Rommel's steel and concrete obstacles on D-Day and beyond.[33]

Two other remarkable scientific and engineering achievements played a critical role in the Pacific theater—but also more generally in the war and therefore are discussed below in separate paragraphs. These were the great medical advances made during the war and the stupendous output of American industry during the war.

Medical Advances

With respect to the Pacific, the great advances in fighting malaria are the most noteworthy of the medical achievements. With the Japanese in control of the sources of quinine, historically the chief antimalarial, it was critical to produce and use synthetic compounds that could provide similar protection.

This was done with the synthesis of Mepacrine, developed by Germany during World War I. In Britain in 1939, only twenty-two pounds were produced. Including production in the United States, total production was raised to 12,500 pounds in 1941 (equivalent to over fifty million tablets), to over one hundred thousand pounds per year by 1943. Along with the production of Mepacrine, it was vital that protocols be adopted and enforced that would require soldiers to take daily doses. At first, many balked at doing this on unfounded fears that the Mepacrine would lead to impotence. The introduction of daily doses of Mepacrine brought a spectacular reduction in the rates of malaria admissions to hospitals at the war fronts. For example, in the British South-East Asia Command, the ratio of malaria admissions to those admitted with wounds was 126:1 in 1943, but by 1944, it had been reduced to 19:1.

In attacking malaria, insecticides also played a significant role, especially DDT. This insecticide was synthesized in Switzerland by Paul Herman Mueller in 1939. It was extraordinarily effective as an insect killer and did not deteriorate when exposed to weathering. Samples were sent to the United States and Germany in late 1942. The United States produced the DDT on a large scale, and it was widely used in the Southeast Asia and Pacific battle theaters against mosquito breeding grounds.

There were other dramatic medical innovations during the war, important in all the theaters of operation. Chief among them was the development of penicillin. This antibiotic, a compound made from the fungus of penicillium notatum, was discovered by

Alexander Fleming in 1928. Little was done to exploit the Fleming discovery, however, until 1938, when Howard Florey and Ernst Chain, at Oxford, began investigating penicillin more systematically and developing ways to produce it in large quantities. Later the United States developed methods to ramp up production to a vast scale. By the time of the D-Day landings in June 1944, there was enough penicillin to treat all casualties requiring it. These later breakthroughs were kept secret, and the Germans never did explore penicillin systematically.[34]

Industrial Output

Finally, the amazing output of the American defense industry was critical in all theaters of the war. In 1941, America produced more steel, aluminum, oil, and motor vehicles than all other major states together. Retooling for defense was done amazingly fast. By illustration, in 1941, America produced 3.5 million passenger cars; from February 1942 until the end of the war, it produced 139 total![35]

In 1942 alone, the United States outproduced all the Axis states together in aircraft, tanks, and heavy guns by almost two to one. During the war, the United States produced three hundred thousand aircraft, over seven thousand naval vessels, and eighty-seven thousand landing craft. By the end of the war, it was producing one long-range bomber an hour[36] at the Willow Run facility near Detroit![37]

Strategic Bombing

The role of Allied strategic bombing and the technical developments that affected it are the subject of chapter 5 and will not be described in any detail here.

In summary, the American and British strategic bombing of Germany (and of satellite and occupied countries) up to 1944 had limited direct effects on German war production but did have significant indirect impacts, largely by diverting substantial resources and armaments from the Eastern Front. In 1944 and 1945, the bombing became increasingly devastating. The human costs of the bombing campaigns were terrible. It has been estimated that the combined Allied bombing offensives killed 400,000–600,000 Germans, largely civilian, and over sixty thousand French citizens and fifty thousand Italians.[38]

The costs were terrible also for the Allies. In the bombing campaigns, the US and British air forces each lost an estimated as much as eighty thousand men. Given such losses, by November 1943, both US and RAF losses in raids deep into Germany looked unsustainable, mainly due to a lack of fighter escorts accompanying the bombers. However, starting in late 1943, there was a dramatic turnaround, due in large part to the introduction into combat of the P-51 Mustang, a fighter with the range to accompany the bombers to Berlin and back. The story of how the Mustang came to be is told in chapter 5.

With the advent of the Mustang, attacks deep into Germany and East Europe in 1944 and 1945 became more devastating, largely destroying the German air force (Luftwaffe), with many of its most decorated pilots killed, in vain attempts to confront the bombers, and also severely impacting German oil production, which was devastating to the German war effort. The reversal of fortune in the skies over Germany came just in time to ensure complete Allied air superiority for the assault on France.

While the Mustang, and other innovations such as the proximity fuse and radar guidance systems were critical technical achievements of the Allies, the Germans also innovated—most dramatically in the development of the unmanned V-2 rocket and the Me-262 jet aircraft, as discussed in chapter 5. But the V-2 program, while an impressive technological achievement, was a tremendous waste of resources. With the Resources poured into the V-2, the US

Strategic Bombing Survey estimated that the Germans could have instead built over twenty-four thousand fighters.[39] The V-2s, largely aimed at London, ended up killing an estimated nine thousand civilians and military personnel and had little impact on the war. The V-2 was undoubtedly the most cost-ineffective weapon of the war.* The Me-262 jet came too late in the war to have much effect, and what effect it did have was limited by a severe lack of oil.

The bombing of noncombatants raises troubling moral questions, which we touch on, though only briefly, in chapter 5. In the end, it may be said that the Allied Combined Bomber Offensive, while it was not always humane, was effective.

D-Day

Throughout 1943 and the early months of 1944, the American and British joint command planned for the invasion of the continent. The challenge was daunting. What had to be launched was the greatest amphibious operation in history against the most strongly defended coastline that any force had ever tried to assault. It was critical that the exact time and place of the invasion be kept secret, that the beach fortifications at the landing sites somehow be dismantled and neutralized, that the ability of the Germans to bring forces to the beachhead be severely degraded, and that means be found to bring supplies to the beachheads rapidly despite there being no natural port that could be used. In all these respects, the Allies succeeded, a story told in chapter 6. As in other aspects of the war, science and technology played prominent roles, as discussed in that chapter.

The invasion commenced in the early morning of June 6, when

---

* An estimated twelve thousand forced laborers were killed producing the V-2—thus making the V-2 a weapon in which more were killed in production than in use against the enemy.

three airborne divisions were parachuted over the Normandy countryside. This was followed, starting at dawn, with the Allies landing five divisions on five beaches the first day.* Despite fierce resistance, especially on Omaha Beach, 155,000 troops were landed on French soil on the first day, including twenty-three thousand airborne forces. The costs were high. On Omaha Beach alone, approximately 2,500 Americans lost their lives. However, by the end of the day, the Allies had taken secure control of a lodgment area sufficient to bring in troops and supplies. By the second week, the Allies had landed half a million troops with attendant equipment, and by July had landed over one million men and nearly two hundred thousand vehicles. In the end, the Allies won a great victory that liberated France and set the stage for the final destruction of Nazi Germany.

The End of the War in Europe

In the several weeks after D-Day, the Allies were able to build up substantial forces. In addition, resistance forces in France undertook large-scale saboteur operations, severely hindering German mobility. But for a time, the Allied forces were not able to break through German defenses away from the beaches. However, in late July, the Allied armies finally broke out, led by General George Patton's Third Army. The Allied armies fanned out across France, taking hundreds of thousands of Germans prisoners. On August 25, Paris was liberated after four years of German occupation. Ernie Pyle, the great war correspondent, wrote: "Paris seems to have all the beautiful girls we have always heard it had ... they dress in riotous colors." The liberation was "the loveliest, brightest story of our time."[40]

The Allies then moved rapidly toward the German border. In

---

* The two most western beaches, Utah and Omaha, were American targets. In the center, Gold was British. To the east, Juno was Canadian, and Sword British.

December 1944, the Germans launched a surprise attack through the Ardennes Forest, initiating the so-called Battle of the Bulge, and for a short time they threatened to cut off some Allied divisions. But this was a last gasp; the Allies shortly regained the initiative. In January, they entered Germany and, facing diminishing German resistance, pushed on toward the heart of Germany.

In the meantime, on June 22, 1944, the third anniversary of the German invasion of Russia, and timed to coordinate with the American/British invasion of France, Russia launched a massive attack on the central Eastern Front, routing the German defenses. In the south also, the Russians broke through the German defenses. On a broad front, Russian armies advanced toward Germany, inflicting over a million casualties, killed, wounded, and captured. The German allies, the Romanians and Bulgarians, upon the approach of the Russians, switched sides. The Hungarians tried also, but the Germans took over for them in a preemptive move. In early 1945, the Russians entered East Prussia, the eastern province of Germany.

Before that, on July 20, there was an assassination attempt on Hitler through a bomb set by Klaus von Stauffenberg, a colonel in the German army, that exploded in Hitler's headquarters in East Prussia. Unfortunately it failed to kill Hitler. The Nazis took savage revenge on the military group behind the action.

In the spring of 1945, American/British armies and the Russian armies marched relentlessly toward the heart of Germany. In March, the Allied armies crossed the Rhine, exploiting a bridge at Remagen that the Germans failed to destroy. A quarter of a million Germans were trapped on the other side of the river. The Allied forces spread out over western Germany, but General Eisenhower decided not to drive toward Berlin, letting the Russians take the city, which Stalin was hell-bent on doing in any case. On April 25, Allied forces approaching from the west and Russian forces approaching from the east converged on the Elbe River, with soldiers of all ranks embracing—a symbolic moment of the forthcoming Allied victory in Europe.

In the drive through Germany, American and British forces discovered the horror of the concentration camps. On April 4, American troops entered part of the Buchenwald camp to find skeletal figures surrounded by unburied corpses. Eleven days later, British troops entered Belsen with its scenes of horror. "The senior officer present ordered a strong attachment of troops to march into the adjacent town of Bergen to bring back the whole population at bayonet point. As they were put to work moving corpses to mass graves, these German civilians all professed shock and protested their ignorance, to the angry disbelief of British officers."[41]

In the east, the Russians drove toward Berlin as German defenses collapsed. By April they were on the outskirts of the city with overwhelming force. On April 30, Hitler killed himself. In the last months of the war, the German generals waged their war with total disregard for the long-range prospects of their people, causing untold destruction for Germans and the Russians alike.[42] In the morning of May 7, at Allied headquarters in France, the chief of staff of the German armed forces high command signed the unconditional surrender documents for all German forces, with all forces set to cease operations at 2300 hours central European time on May 8; on May 9, the German high command signed a similar document in Berlin, explicitly surrendering to Soviet forces. The war in Europe had ended with the unconditional surrender of Germany.*

The Atomic Bomb and the End of the War

Chapter 7 tells the story of the Manhattan Project, the most famous and at the end the most impactful of the scientific advances during the war. Fission was discovered in December 1938 by Otto Hahn

---

* V-E day for the western Allies is May 8. For the Soviet Union, it is May 9.

and Fritz Strassmann in Germany and explained shortly afterward by Lise Meitner in Sweden and her nephew, Otto Frisch, then working in Denmark. Meitner had been a colleague of Hahn but had been forced to leave Germany because she was Jewish.

When a neutron strikes a uranium nucleus, the nucleus sometimes splits into two smaller nuclei recoiling from the collision with tremendous energy. When physicists in the United States, Britain, France, Germany, and Russia heard of this discovery, they immediately looked to see if, in the fission event, more than one neutron is emitted. If that were true, a chain reaction might be possible, though even were it so, whether an atomic bomb could actually be constructed was far from clear. As it turned out, between two and three neutrons are emitted with each fission.

This so alarmed a few American and British scientists that they agitated for their countries to initiate research to see if a bomb was possible. A key breakthrough in understanding was made by two Jewish émigré scientists at Birmingham University in England, Frisch (who had moved from Denmark) and Rudolph Peierls. In March 1940, the two physicists wrote a short memorandum outlining how a bomb could be built. The memorandum galvanized programs in the United States and Britain. In the United States, it evolved into the Manhattan Project.

The key tasks of the Manhattan Project were first to build a reactor that could achieve a chain reaction. This was done by a team at the University of Chicago under the direction of the great Italian physicist, Enrico Fermi. The chain reaction was achieved in December 1942. Secondly, efforts were mounted to produce enough fissile material for a bomb—highly enriched uranium (HEU) and plutonium. A bomb must include at least one of these materials. Neither fissile material existed in nature, and it would take a herculean effort to produce sufficient material for even one bomb in time to affect the outcome of the war. HEU was produced at Oak Ridge, Tennessee, and plutonium in large reactors built at Hanford,

Washington. The work to design a bomb was done at Los Alamos, New Mexico, under the inspired direction of J. Robert Oppenheimer.

On July 16, 1945, after the war in Europe had ended, the first atomic bomb was detonated in the New Mexico desert, at Alamagordo. It was a plutonium bomb and had the explosive force equivalent to about twenty thousand tons of TNT. The bomb dropped on Nagasaki on August 9 was a plutonium bomb. A simpler design using HEU did not have to be tested, and this was the design of the bomb dropped on Hiroshima on August 6.

The race for the bomb in the United States was in large part galvanized by a fear that the Germans were also working toward a bomb. The German effort was under the direction of Werner Heisenberg, a Nobel winner, but it operated at a far lesser scale than the American effort; and by early 1945, the Allies ascertained that the Germans were not close to a weapon. Nevertheless, the atomic program moved forward unabated, and the possible use of the bomb now became focused on Japan.

The United States determined that when the bombs were ready, they should be used against Japan to shock it into surrender. As noted, the bombs were dropped on Hiroshima and Nagasaki on August 6 and 9. Japan surrendered unconditionally on August 11. Some historians argue that Japan was near to surrender in any case, and especially so after the Soviet Union launched an attack on Japan on August 8. But surely the atomic bombs contributed to the surrender.

Bibliography

Atkinson, Rick. *The Guns at Last Light.* Henry Holt and Company, 2013.

Beevor, Antony. *The Second World War.* Back Bay Books, 2012.

Brown, Anthony Cave. *Bodyguard of Lies.* Quill/William Morrow, 1975.

Buderi, Robert. *The Invention that Changed the World.* Simon and Schuster, 1996.

Evans, Richard. *The Third Reich at War.* Penguin, 2009.

Hartcup, Guy. *The Effect of Science in the Second World War.* Palgrave, 2003.

Hastings, Max. *All Hell Let Loose: The World at War 1939–1945.* Harper Press, 2011.

Hess, Gary. *The United States at War, 1941–1945.* Wiley-Blackwell, 2011.

Jones, R.V. *Most Secret War.* Hamish Hamilton, 1978.

Kennedy, Paul. *Engineers of Victory.* Random House, 2013.

Kershaw, Ian. *Fateful Choices: Ten Decisions that Changed the World, 1940–1941.* Penguin Books, 2008.

Klein, Maury. *A Call to Arms: Mobilizing America for World War II.* Bloomsbury Press, 2013.

McIntyre, Ben. *Double Cross: The True Story of D-Day Spies.* Broadway Books, 2013.

McIntyre, Ben. *Operation Mincemeat: How a Dead Man and a Bizarre Plan Fooled the Nazis and Assured an Allied Victory.* Broadway Books, 2011.

Murray, Williamson, and Allan Millett. *A War To Be Won.* Belknap Press, 2000.

Olson, Lynne. *Those Angry Days: Roosevelt, Lindbergh, and American Fight Over World War II, 1939–1941.* Random House, 2014.

Olson, Lynne. *Last Hope Island: Britain, Occupied Europe, and the Brotherhood that Helped Turn The Tide of War.* Random House, 2017.

Overy, Richard. *Why the Allies Won.* Pimlico, 2006.

Overy, Richard. *The Bombers and the Bombed.* Viking, 2013.

Rhodes, Richard. *The Making of the Atomic Bomb.* Simon and Schuster, 1986.

Symons, Craig. *The Battle of Midway.* Oxford University Press, 2011.

Wilmot, Chester. *The Struggle for Europe.* Harper and Brothers, 1952.

Film:

Why We Fight—seven films directed by Frank Capra, commissioned by the US government to show to servicemen, and later shown in theaters across the country—available online.

CHAPTER 2

---— ⚛ ——---

The Battle of Britain: Radar and the Spitfire

The Setting

In the perilous summer of 1940, Britain stood virtually alone against the Nazi menace. Not fully alone since several invaluable assets came to Britain from the occupied countries of Europe, cryptographers and pilots from Poland, merchant ships from Norway, Queen Wilhemina from the Netherlands, King Haakon from Norway, Charles DeGaulle and eventually the Free French from France, spies from several of the occupied countries, and others.[43] But the moment was perilous for the British. The Nazi blitzkrieg had overrun Poland in September 1939 and by June 1940 had conquered Norway, Denmark, the Netherlands, Belgium, and France. Russia, at that time, was an ally of Hitler. And the United States was neutral, with a large fraction of its population hoping that it could stay out of the European war. Hitler at first thought that Britain would sue for peace—and when it did not, he considered an invasion across the English Channel, operation Sea-Lion. Some dispute how seriously this was considered by the German military—but, whatever Germany's ultimate aims were, Germany had to have control of the air to make an invasion possible. From July to September 1940, the Germans sent waves of bombers over England to attack shipping, airfields, factories producing fighter aircraft, and other targets. To combat these attacks, the British had antiaircraft fire—but, above all, fighter aircraft to attack the German bombers and their fighter escorts. Thus, the Battle of Britain. The stakes of the outcome of this battle were infinite, as memorably expressed by British Prime Minister Winston Churchill in a series of great speeches.

Churchill to the House of Commons, June 4, 1940:

> Even though large tracts of Europe and many old and famous States have fallen or may fall into the grip of the Gestapo and all the odious apparatus of Nazi rule, we shall not flag or fail. We shall go on to the end. We shall fight in France, we shall fight on the seas and oceans, we shall fight with growing confidence and growing strength in the air, we shall defend our island, whatever the cost may be. We shall fight on the beaches, we shall fight on the landing grounds, we shall fight in the fields and in the streets, we shall fight in the hills; we shall never surrender, and even if, which I do not for a moment believe, this island or a large part of it were subjugated and starving, then our Empire beyond the seas, armed and guarded by the British Fleet, would carry on the struggle, until, in God's good time, the new world, with all its power and might, steps forth to the rescue and the liberation of the old.

Churchill to the House of Commons, June 18, 1940:

> What General Weygand has called the Battle of France is over. I expect that the Battle of Britain is about to begin. Upon this battle depends the survival of Christian civilisation. Upon it depends

our own British life, and the long continuity of our institutions and our Empire. The whole fury and might of the enemy must very soon be turned on us. Hitler knows that he will have to break us in this island or lose the war. If we can stand up to him, all Europe may be freed and the life of the world may move forward into broad, sunlit uplands.

But if we fail, then the whole world, including the United States, including all that we have known and cared for, will sink into the abyss of a new dark age made more sinister, and perhaps more protracted, by the lights of perverted science. Let us therefore brace ourselves to our duties, and so bear ourselves, that if the British Empire and its Commonwealth last for a thousand years, men will still say, *This* was their finest hour.

In the air battle to come, many factors would play a role: the skill and courage of the airmen on both sides, the tactics used, the numbers and quality of the aircraft on each side, and technology. In the words of Len Deighton, "In the late 19th century and the early 20th, three inventions changed the world—the internal combustion engine, the air plane, and wireless communication. The Battle of Britain was fought and decided by these three inventions alone unlike any other battle in history."[44]

For the British, two factors were of critical importance—radar and the Spitfire single-engine fighter. Where did these come from? To answer that, we have to go back to the days before the war.

The Beginning of Radar in Britain

Countries experienced bombing from the air for the first time during WWI. In Britain, German bombing killed fewer than 1,500 and injured some 3,400, far too few to affect the path of the war but enough to point to the dangers of the future.[45]

By the 1930s, the dread of bombing was widespread, and it haunted the imagination of many statesmen, especially in Britain. Its most famous expression was in a much-quoted speech to the House of Commons in 1932 by Stanley Baldwin, soon to become prime minister:

> I think it is well for the man in the street to realize that there is no power on earth than can protect him from being bombed. Whatever people may tell him, the bomber will always get through.[46]

British concerns grew even more urgent with the advent to power in Germany of Hitler and the Nazis. But not everyone in Britain was convinced that "the bomber will always get through."

In 1934, the director of scientific research at the Air Ministry, Henry Wimperis, appointed a committee to investigate whether and how a successful defense network could somehow in some way be developed. The committee was chaired by Henry Tizard, then chairman of Britain's Aeronautical Research Committee. In parallel, Wimperis sought to explore whether a death ray could be developed—a weapon that could kill, say, a bomber pilot, through radio waves or other radiation from afar. And to help him think through this possibility, he asked Robert Watson-Watt to consider the problem. Watson-Watt, a short, somewhat portly Scot with an ebullient manner, was superintendent of the National Physical Laboratory, where he had been studying radio waves interacting with the ionosphere.[47]

Watson-Watt and a colleague quickly worked out that a death ray was not remotely possible at that time. They looked more precisely on whether radio waves could raise the temperature of eight pints of water from 98°F to 105°F from a distance of five miles—that is, could the blood of a bomber pilot be so heated? In reporting their negative result to the Tizard Committee, Watson-Watt noted, however, that while a death ray was impractical, "meanwhile attention is being turned to the still difficult, but less unpromising problem of radio-detection opposed to radio-destruction." The committee seized on this thought and asked Watson-Watt to explore the idea further, which he did in an historic memo to the committee on February 12, 1935.[48]

In this memo, Watson-Watt first noted that emissions directly by the aircraft would not allow reliable detection. For example, sound, say from the engine, has too much competing noise and also travels too slowly. Infrared radiation generated by the heat of the engine also would not work well; water in the atmosphere absorbs too much of the radiation.

But, with an antenna, radio waves could to some extent be directed. Upon striking a metallic surface, such as an aircraft, some of the radio waves would be reflected and sent back to a sensitive receiver at the same site at which the signal was sent out, or conceivably at a different site. Radio waves are a form of electromagnetic radiation and travel with the speed of light—300,000 kilometers per second! If the radio waves are sent out in pulses, the time for a pulse to get reflected back would tell how far away the plane was. For example, say a plane is some unknown distance away, and a radio pulse is sent out and gets back in two milliseconds (two one-thousands of a second). That means that it took the pulse one millisecond to reach the plane (and of course one millisecond to return). Since radio waves travel at 300,000 kilometers per second, this would means that the plane was three hundred kilometers (or about 180 miles) away.

In addition to the great speed of radio waves, their other great advantage is that the waves can travel through darkness, cloud, or fog.[49] With back-of-the-envelope calculations, Watson-Watt, in the memorandum, showed how such detection of enemy bombers would be possible.[50]

The Watson-Watt memorandum excited the Tizard Committee. But the person in charge of funding development of the concept, Air Marshall Hugh Dowding, then air member for research and development, first demanded a demonstration. The showdown was set for February 26, 1935. The Watson-Watt team scrounged together a crude transmitter and put together a receiver and cathode-ray display at a nearby airfield. The following morning, observers crowded around the display as a Heyford bomber made several passes over the airfield at about ten thousand feet. On first pass, the cathode-ray tube showed little, but on subsequent passes, the marker on the cathode-ray tube began to glow.[51] Dowding needed no further proof and became a strong supporter of radar development. As we shall see later, Dowding soon after in 1936 was appointed director of fighter defense.

Fig. 2.1 Robert Watson-Watt—Founder of British Radar
(Courtesy of Imperial War Museum)

This was the birth of British radio detection finding (RDF) as the British called it. Later, in 1940, the US Navy gave it the name "radar," standing for RAdio Detection And Ranging, a term the British later adopted and that we will use from now on. It is fitting that "radar" is a palindrome, a word that is the same forward and backward, mimicking the idea of a pulse going out and being reflected back.

The idea of radar was already in the air. The German scientist Heinrich Hertz, who in 1887 first used a spark gap to generate electromagnetic waves, was already aware that radio waves reflect from solid objects and indeed had even demonstrated this.[52] As early as 1904, a German engineer had filed a patent for a collision prevention device for ships using reflected radio waves. Both in the United States and in Britain, scientists in the 1920s had set up experiments that measured the height of the ionosphere by sending up radio pulses and timing the return.[53] And by the mid-1930s, scientists in the United States, Italy, France, the Soviet Union, and Germany were discovering that aircraft and ships could be detected by radio waves out to tens of miles. But it was the British that first undertook to develop a mature radar system designed to give early warning of incoming aircraft.[54]

The Age of Wireless

Electromagnetic waves were first explained and predicted by the great British scientist James Clerk Maxwell, who worked out their character from years of experiments by Michael Faraday in Britain, Joseph Henry in the United States, and many others. The phenomena of electromagnetism derive from the tremendous force exerted between two charged particles, say for example, two electrons—a billion, billion, billion, billion times greater than the gravitational force between the particles. Unlike gravity, charged particles come in two forms—positive and negative. Two charges of the same kind repel, and two charges of different kind attract. In much of nature, the positive and negative charges are in almost complete balance. If they were not, the forces would be stupendous. Richard Feynman, a famed twentieth-century physicist, made vivid this fact of nature:

> If you were standing at arms length from someone and each of you had one percent more electrons than protons, the repelling force would be incredible. How great? Enough to lift the empire state building? No! To lift Mount Everest? No! The repulsion would be enough to lift a "weight" equal to that of the entire earth![55]

Maxwell postulated that the speed of electromagnetic waves is "c"—the speed of light that had been previously measured; he then concluded that light itself must be an electromagnetic wave, as in fact it is. Again one might quote Feynman on the greatness of Maxwell's achievement:

> From the long view of history of mankind … there can be little doubt that the most significant event of the 19th century will be judged as Maxwell's discovery of the laws of electrodynamics. The American Civil War will pale into provincial insignificance in comparison with the important scientific event of the same decade.[56]

In 1887, the aforementioned Heinrich Hertz showed how sparks can generate electric waves and in a series of experiments confirmed Maxwell's theory. An electric current generates a magnetic field, and a time varying magnetic field generates an electric field. A field is a pretty abstract concept. What it means is that if there is charge, q, moving with velocity **v** at some point in space, there will be a force acting on the charge given by the formula:

$\mathbf{F} = q(\mathbf{E} + \mathbf{v} \times \mathbf{B})$, where **F**, **E**, **v**, and **B** are so-called vectors—that is, they have a direction in space. **E** and **B** are the electric and magnetic fields. And even if there is no charge present, we could think of an electric field, **E**, and a magnetic field **B** at each point in space.[57] The vector cross product, **v** x **B**, equals the absolute value of **v** times the absolute value of **B** times the sine of the angle between them with a direction perpendicular to both **v** and **B**. The direction is given by the so-called right-hand rule—imagine a hand out as if to shake someone with two fingers representing the two vectors pointing straight and to the left, then the thumb would be straight up.

v x **B** = IvI x IBI x $\sin\theta$ **n**,
where **n** is a unit vector perpendicular to both **v** and **B**.

If **v** and **B** are in the same direction or opposite, $\sin\theta = 0$. The maximum force would be if they are at right angles to each other.

Electromagnetic waves travel with the velocity of light and consist of magnetic and electric fields that are at right angles to each other and also at right angles to the direction of travel.[58] One half of the energy contained in the wave is in the form of electric energy, and one half in the form of magnetic energy. The radio waves produced by an alternating current will vary sinusoidally in intensity with the frequency of the current and will be alternatively positive and negative. The strength of the radio wave is measured by the voltage (energy potential) produced in space by the electric field of the wave, usually expressed in microvolts per meter. Every electrical circuit carrying alternating current radiates a certain amount of electrical energy in the form of electromagnetic waves, but the amount of energy thus radiated is extremely small unless all the dimensions of the circuit approach the order of magnitude of a wavelength. Thus long wavelength waves require a large antenna system for effective radiation.[59]

Electromagnetic waves are characterized by their frequency or wavelength, always remembering that the product of the frequency and wavelength is the speed of light, c. So the higher the frequency, the shorter the wavelength. Relatively low frequency waves are those used for radio. Much higher frequency waves that our optical nerves could detect are the light waves, and still higher frequency waves are termed x-rays and gamma rays. The waves with frequency a little lower than light waves are infrared waves, and those a little higher are ultraviolet. See figure 2.2. Radar during WWII worked on wavelengths generally between three centimeters and fifty meters—that is on frequencies between ten billion and six million cycles per second. The lower wavelength (microwave) radars, however, did not come until later in the war. During the Battle of Britain, it was the longer wavelengths that played the critical role.

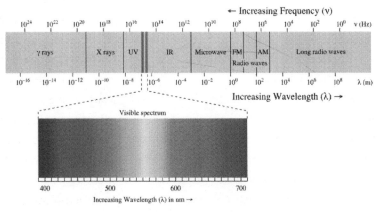

Fig. 2.2 Electromagnetic Spectrum

Elements of a Radar System[60]

The elements of a radar system are the transmitter, modulator, duplexer, and receiver. The transmitter puts an electric current through a conductor or antenna. The power radiated is proportional to the product of the voltage and current. As noted, it is important that the dimensions of the antenna are comparable to the wavelength of the radio waves generated. Thus, for example, a twenty-foot aerial carrying a current of frequency six million vibrations per second (wavelength fifty meters) would radiate energy efficiently.

The modulator generates pulses of high power but short duration. Typically, pulse lengths lie in the range 0.1–10 microseconds (0.1–10 millionth of a second); and the repetition frequency lies in the range 200–10,000 cycles. Thus the duty cycle of a transmitter producing one-microsecond pulses at a rate of a thousand per second is "on" for 0.001 sec. The average power then for a peak power output of 500 KW is 500 watts. The duplexer isolates the sensitive receiver from the damaging effects of the high-power transmitter pulses when the same antenna is used for transmission and reception.

The receiver incorporates an antenna, such that when the incoming radio wave transits the antenna, a voltage is created across the antenna. In many radars, the receiving antenna is the same as the transmitting antenna. Any antenna capable of radiating electrical energy is also able to absorb energy from a passing radio wave. This occurs because the electromagnetic flux of the wave, in cutting across the antenna conductor, induces in the antenna a voltage that varies with time in exactly the same way as does the current flowing in the antenna radiating the wave. The induced voltage, in association with the current that it produces, represents energy that is absorbed from the passing wave.[61]

A cathode ray tube could then record the received pulses. Such a tube has three major components—a so-called electron gun that focuses a beam of electrons coming off a cathode, a means of deflecting the beam—electrostatically or magnetically, and a fluorescent screen upon which the electron beam is focused to form a fine spot giving off light when bombarded by electrons.[62]

The performance of the radar may be characterized by the power received at the antenna upon reflection from the target, P_r. It is given by this equation:

$$P_r = (P_tGS) A/(4\pi)^2 d^4$$

Where P_t = the power of the transmitter, S = the cross section of the target, A = the effective area of the antenna, G = antenna gain, and d = distance to target. For a fighter plane, the S might be about ten square meters; a bomber might be 150 square meters.[63] The gain equals $4\pi A/\lambda^2$ and one may assume for simplicity that the gain in transmission is the same as gain in reception, which would be the case if the same antenna is used for both. The gain, and thus directivity of the radar beam, would be much greater for the shorter wavelengths.

It may immediately be seen that to double the range of the radar, one would have to increase the power transmitted sixteen-fold.

When the same antenna is used for transmission and reception, the gain in transmission = gain in reception.

Chain Home

The Tizard Committee upon receiving the Watson-Watt memorandum was immediately taken with the concept of radar and quickly established under the direction of Watson-Watt a research group located about ninety miles from London to pursue the idea further. The critical tasks were (1) to increase the power of the outgoing waves, (2) to increase the Gain—the directivity of the radio wave beam, and (3) to increase the sensitivity of the receiver. Schemes were developed to measure the direction of the incoming bombers and their altitude. The aircraft's speed of approach could be found by comparing the computed ranges at different times.

Development proceeded rapidly. By the outbreak of war in 1939, a set of twenty-one radar stations were established along the British coast, with a tower roughly every twenty-five miles of coastline. Each station consisted of transmitters lodged on three or four steel towers, 360 feet high. The antennas were strung over tower platforms fifty, two hundred, and 350 feet off the ground. The result was a signal directed forward along the perpendicular to the line of the tower. The receivers were lodged on separate 240-foot towers a few hundred meters away. The power of the transmitters was initially 360 kilowatts, and this was later increased to 750 kilowatts. The antenna system was devised to put out a reasonably narrow beam at ten meters wavelength, and measures were adopted to allow the radar operators to measure both the altitude of the bombers and their azimuth (that is, direction). The system at that stage could not reliably detect low-flying aircraft because of clutter reflected from the Channel; and the Chain Home was supplemented then by another set of stations operating at 1.5 meters wavelength termed Chain Home Low. These sets with more narrow beams had antennas that rotated to scan the entire horizon, and they produced less clutter from the sea. The Chain Home system stretched across the eastern shoreline of the British Isles, looking outward, offering almost continuous coverage over the English Channel. By the time of the Battle of Britain, Chain Home was further expanded to cover the west coast and Northern Ireland.[64]

The theoretical detection range of the Chain Home stations was two hundred miles, but the practical average detection range was eighty miles. For Chain Home Low, the detection range was about thirty miles.

Radar could not yet work over land, given all the clutter from hills and dales, and it had to be supplemented by persons on rooftops searching the skies. At the outbreak of war, there were thirty thousand observers reporting to central air defense headquarters.

Along with the fighters, the British air defense also relied on antiaircraft guns to cover the entire country. By June 1940, there were over one thousand heavy and five hundred light guns.[65]

Along with this scientific and engineering work, Tizard and Dowding realized that detecting enemy bombers would do no good unless the information could be used to direct fighters to intercept the bombers. And it may be said that the great achievement of British radar was not in the Chain Home radar stations themselves but in the way the information was interpreted and used.[66]

During the Battle of Britain, the heart of the British system of defense lay at command HQ at Bentley Priory in Stanmore, on the outskirts of London. Information on incoming aircraft was relayed by landline from all the radar stations around the coast. The plots were laid out on a large map table, and once the aircraft track was clearly established, the information was relayed to group HQ and to the individual airfields. Once airborne, aircraft were directed by radio to intercept the observed bombers coming over the channel. Also procedures were developed for IFF, Identification Friend or Foe.

In the command bunker, locations of both friendly and enemy aircraft formations were displayed on a large map table using numbered blocks. These counters—red for enemy, black for friendly— had numbers to show estimated altitude and strength, with an arrow to indicate direction.[67] Young women in the Women's Royal Naval Service (Wrens) were adept at managing the map-board display. The plots were passed to operations rooms at sector, group, and fighter command headquarters. At each place, the map table would be identical. From a balcony, the whole map table was watched. Also available to the controller and staff on the balcony was a board fitted with colored lights. It showed at a glance what squadrons were available in thirty minutes, which were at readiness (five minutes) or at cockpit readiness (two minutes), and which were in the air.[68, 69]

So radar came just in time for the British. And so did, it turned out, the Spitfire, which in the mid-1930s wedded the innovative Rolls-Royce Merlin PV-12 aeroengine with the path-breaking airframe design of Reginald Mitchell.

Fig. 2.3 Chain Home Radar (Courtesy of Imperial War Museum)

Fig. 2.4 Radar Map Room Operated by Members of the Women's Royal
Navy Service (WRENS) (Courtesy of Imperial War Museum)

The Spitfire

The Battle of Britain opposed German bombers and accompanying fighters against the British fighters and ground antiaircraft. The principal German bombers were the Heinkel 111 and the Stuka dive-bombers.

The Spitfire was one of the three metal monoplane (single wing) fighters that dominated the air battles in the Battle of Britain. The others were the Hurricane and the German Messerschmitt Bf-109.[70] While the Hurricane, designed by Sydney Camm, and the Bf-109 were excellent fighters and played salient roles in the coming battle, our focus will be on the Spitfire.

How Planes Fly

Four forces work on an airplane: gravity pulling the plane down to earth; lift that causes the air pressure above the wing to be less than below due to the shape of the wing and its attack through the atmosphere; drag, caused by air buildup in front of the plane as it moves forward; and thrust, the force of the engine pushing air past the rapidly rotating propellers, causing a kind of horizontal "lift" forward.

The biplanes used in World War I sought to maximize lift by utilizing two wings—though doubling the wing area did not double the lift since to some extent the wings interfered with each other; also the double wings created extra drag. The biplanes were hopelessly slow compared to the monoplanes. Though they had a shorter turning radius, the speed of the monoplanes completely outclassed them in combat.

The Merlin PV-12 Aeroengine

Thrust is provided by the aeroengine, and here progress during the 1930s was rapid. The best of the engines were the Daimler-Benz DB 601A in Germany and the Merlin PV-12 in Great Britain. The Merlin was designed and built by Rolls-Royce.[71] The critical designer was Henry Royce, one of the great engineering geniuses of the twentieth century, who conceived of an engine that would power an extremely fast, high-altitude fighter. Royce, who had made his name initially from the production of famously high-quality auto engines, in ill health much of his life, worked tirelessly on new aeroengine designs until his death in 1933. He left behind an impressive design team that carried on the work.

Rolls-Royce had the habit of naming its aeroengines after the swift raptors of the sky, and the name "Merlin" was not a reference to the great wizard but rather to one of the fiercest of the falcons. The Merlin fitted both to the Hurricane and the Spitfire was a 12-cylinder, water-cooled engine, weighing 1,300 pounds and producing 1,050 pounds of thrust. The engine converts rotational energy into a propulsive force or thrust driving air past the rapidly spinning propellers. In a story told in chapter 5, the Merlin also played a critical role in strategic bombing when it was married to the Mustang airframe.[72]

The Design of the Spitfire

During 1934, the British Air Ministry was responding to intelligence reports of the secret German air force. Demand for better RAF fighters was urgent.

In 1928, the Supermarine aircraft company was bought by the giant Vickers-Armstrong concern, perhaps mostly to acquire Supermarine's brilliant design department, headed by Reginald

Mitchell. Mitchell, though severely ailing, had visited Germany in 1933 and became convinced that war was coming. He then became obsessed with developing the best fighter possible and worked tirelessly to achieve that aim.

The Spitfire was original in every way, perhaps most markedly by its elliptical wings, incredibly thin yet strong enough to mount eight machine guns and to allow high-gravity turns. Mitchell designed the aircraft from the beginning with promise of the PV-12 Merlin engine. The engine had its own teething problems and was not ready until 1936. When it was wedded with the Mitchell airframe, the Spitfire was born. It was a close-run thing! As noted, Royce died in 1933, still working on his deathbed on the newer engine design, and Mitchell died in 1937 at the age of forty-two. He lived long enough to see the first test flights of his Spitfire.

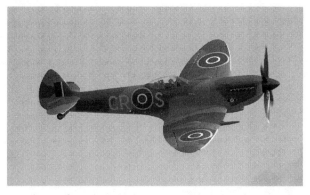

Fig. 2.5 The Spitfire: The British Interceptor that played a critical role in the Battle of Britain was a result of the marriage of an airframe design by Reginald Mitchell and an aeroengine designed by Henry Royce.

Fighters Compared

The Bf-109 designed by Messerschmitt was an extremely good fighter, somewhat better than the Hurricane, and in some critical respects inferior to the Spitfire. Visibility—life and death for combat flyers—was incomparably better in the Spitfire. The bubble-shaped hood gave headroom and a chance to see down, up, and around. The 109 hood had thick bars like a prison, and it sometimes touched the top of the helmet.[73]

Once airborne, the Spitfires most often took on the German fighters, and the Hurricanes generally the German bombers. The Spitfires stayed at relatively high altitude, while the Hurricanes dropped down to where the German bombers were.

The Battle of Britain

Thus by July 1940, the stage was set for the great air battle soon to begin between the German Luftwaffe and the Royal Air Force (RAF).

During much of the Battle, July to September 1940, the number of fighters and pilots was roughly equivalent. Thus, by August 1940, when the Germans launched their heaviest attacks on Britain, the British had 1,032 fighters in the operational force, with 715 ready for immediate operation. The Hurricanes accounted for 55 percent of the operational aircraft, the Spitfire, 31 percent. The Germans then had 1,011 fighters, with 805 ready for immediate operation.[74]

Despite the rough equivalence of fighters, Germany had more bombers and dive-bombers and also could concentrate attacks on southern England, while the British had to defend in the north as well. So in specific confrontations, the RAF could be badly outnumbered in total aircraft. However, in aircraft production, the British were outstripping the Germans. During the summer and autumn of 1940, the Germans produced 775 Bf-109s against 1,900 Hurricane and Spitfire fighters produced in Britain.[75]

The German effort was orchestrated by Reichsmarshall Herman Goering, commander in chief of the Luftwaffe, a confidant of Hitler and, in 1940, the second most powerful person in Germany. The key person in Britain was Air Chief Marshall,

Sir Hugh Dowding, commander in chief of Fighter Command, appointed to that position in 1936. Dowding, who as member for Research and Development was responsible for overseeing the development of the Spitfire and the Chain Home system, was now ready to take these weapons to war. He was critical in husbanding British fighters for the upcoming battle. Dowding at the start of the war was fifty-nine years old, a ski champion but with a reserved, acerbic personality. He was opposed by many in the British Air Ministry, who were fixated on the importance of the bombers and wanted Britain to produce more of them at the expense of expanding the fighter fleet. Others wanted to send fighters to France after the German invasion, and though many fighters were thrown into the battles in France, Dowding succeeded in limiting the numbers so committed. (Dowding's son became a Spitfire pilot just in time for the battle to come.[76])

Fig. 2.6 Sir Hugh Dowding—Commander in Chief of Fighter Command during the Battle of Britain (Courtesy of Imperial War Museum)

The battle might be divided into four phases:[77]

Phase one: starting in July, there was a month of attacks on British coastal convoys and air battles over the channel.

Phase two: from August 12, the eve of Adlertag (Eagle Day), to about August 23 came the main German assault on a whole range of targets.

Phase three: from August 20 to September 6, RAF fighter fields in southeast England were priority objectives.

Phase four: from September 7 to the end of the year, the attacks centered on London, first by day and then later by night. This was the blitz.

Phase One

In phase one, German attacks on shipping were effective, and Dowding was under pressure to commit more fighters to defense—but he refused to draw his fighters in a large way into the conflict. During this period, radar became increasingly effective; the women looking at the radar blips were able to identify large incoming German attacks.

On August 7, German intelligence issued this secret report to the operational commands:

> As the British fighters are controlled from the ground by radio telephone, their forces are tied to their respective ground stations and are thereby restricted in mobility, even taking into consideration the probability that the ground stations are partly mobile. Consequently, the assembly of strong fighter forces at determined points and at short notice is not to be expected.[78]

It was a disastrous error of judgment, completely ignoring the impact of radar.

Phase Two

From Eagle Day on, the German attacks were on a scale far exceeding all previous attacks. For example, on Thursday, August 12, the Germans flew 1,786 sorties and 1,700 the next day and night!

However, despite the weight of attacks, German strategy and tactics were indecisive. No clear priority lists were made: shipping, airfields, radar installations, Rolls-Royce and Spitfire manufacturing, and so on. The German attacks were not well conceived. The German surely knew that the Hurricanes and Spitfires were powered by Rolls-Royce engines; and there were only two places where they were being made. And the Spitfire was even more vulnerable, for there was only one factory in fulltime airframe production, and that was at the well-known Supermarine factory in Southampton. Yet German attacks were not focused on these seemingly obvious targets.[79]

On August 15, German bomber losses were severe, and it at last became clear that without fighter protection, bombers could not get through without suffering large losses. This led Goering to decree that given the severity of the bomber losses, henceforth each bomber should be accompanied by three fighters. He also noted that:

> "It is doubtful whether there is any point to continuing attacks on radar sites, in view of the fact that not one of those attacked has so far been put out of action."[80]

It was one of the greatest errors of the war.

Phase Three

The Germans were now using radar devices of their own to allow more precision bombing at night. The systems, named Knickebein and X-Gerat, used radio beams from stations on the continent to guide the bombers over their targets. The British to some degree were able to jam the beams, especially the Knickebein, and confuse the bombers but not completely so.[81] (This is discussed in slightly more detail in chapter 5.)

By September 1, many of the British airfields were badly damaged.[82] The Germans at last appeared close to achieving air superiority over southeast England for the invasion. But fate intervened. In retaliation to some sporadic British bombing of Berlin, Hitler on September 7 suddenly demanded terror raids on London, diverting the bombers from their attacks on the RAF airfields. Though causing grievous casualties on Londoners, this saved the day for the RAF.

Phase Four

The bombing of London continued unabated during the first weeks of September, causing great damage (the blitz on Britain ultimately killed forty thousand people) but also leading to large losses of bombers. On September 15—now celebrated as Battle of Britain Day—over two hundred Spitfires and Hurricanes were over London; twice that day, three hundred fighters were over the southern counties. The Germans threw one hundred bombers guarded by four hundred fighters at London. The RAF claimed 180 planes shot down, instead of the sixty credited after the war, but what was important is that the Germans became convinced that they could not get air superiority anytime soon.

On September 17, British intelligence intercepted a secret radio message—Hitler officially decided to postpone operation Sea-Lion (invasion of Britain). The Luftwaffe was also exhausted by the summer battles. The bomber units were depleted and their morale low. "The Luftwaffe turned its attentions to the techniques of night bombing and Hitler turned to maps of Russia."[83]

Conclusion

Hitler called off Sea-Lion on September 17, and there was never any attempt to repeat it.[84]

In the Battle of Britain, British application of science and technology, above all in their development of a remarkable and effective radar network through the integration of scientists and military at the highest levels, was outstanding. It was an achievement repeated throughout the war where the Allied integration of science and technology into the war effort far surpassed German efforts.[85]

Just by remaining intact, Fighter Command had won the Battle of Britain. Dowding had only to keep September's skies too dangerous for a German invasion in order to force a postponement to 1941 or indefinitely—and this he did. By forestalling invasion, Britain convinced the United States that it was in the war for keeps and would never surrender, and it may have also helped to persuade Hitler to launch an invasion of the Soviet Union; once the Soviet Union was defeated, Hitler reasoned Britain would then surely have to sue for peace.

Thus, the Battle of Britain was a critical turning point in the war, though in comparison to later battles, it was sharply limited. Indeed before the war ended, the Luftwaffe was to lose in one day the same number of planes it lost in the entire summer of 1940![86]

Churchill in a speech to House of Commons on August 20:

> The gratitude of every home in our Island, in our
> Empire, and indeed throughout the world, except

in the abodes of the guilty, goes out to the British airmen who, undaunted by odds, unwearied in their constant challenge and mortal danger, are turning the tide of the World War by their prowess and by their devotion. *Never in the field of human conflict was so much owed by so many to so few.* All our hearts go out to the fighter pilots, whose brilliant actions we see with our own eyes day after day ...

Bibliography

Beevor, Antony. *The Second World War*, chapter 8. Back Bay Books, 2012.

Bowen, E.G. *Radar Days*. Adam Hilger, 1987.

Buderi, Robert. *The Invention that Changed the World*. Simon and Schuster, 1996.

Deighton, Len. *Fighter*. Castle Books, 2000.

Hartcup, Guy. *The Effect of Science on the Second World War*, chapter 2. Palgrave, 2003.

Olson, Lynne. *Last Hope Island*. Random House, 2017.

Overy, Richard. *The Battle of Britain*. W.W. Norton, 2002.

Terman, Frederick E. *Electronic and Radio Engineering*, McGraw-Hill, 1955.

CHAPTER 3

⚛

Breaking Enigma

Radio Communication and Cryptography

At the start of WWII, with militaries increasingly using radio communication, such that adversaries could listen in to the communications as well as the units receiving and sending messages, cryptography took on sudden importance. Each country sought the most secure code system possible, and each sought to break the enemy's system.

The challenge may be stated simply. Hans wants to send a secret message to Fritz. The enemy, Tommy, can listen in. So Hans adopts a key such that the plaintext message is encrypted. Fritz, knowing the key, can then decrypt the message and recover the plaintext. Tommy, without knowing the key, will see the encrypted message but will not be able to decipher it—or so Hans and Fritz hope.

One straightforward encryption strategy, in use by countries and persons for over two thousand years, is simply to transpose one letter for another—this is called monoalphabetic substitution. For example, the so-called Caesar's cipher transposes each letter in the plaintext three places up the alphabet, so that A becomes D, B becomes E, and so on. Thus the plaintext message, "See you at six" becomes VHH BRX DW VLA. Unfortunately for the folks doing the encryption, such a substitution pattern is relatively easy to break, by dint of frequency analysis, if enough encrypted text is intercepted. In English, the letter *e* is the most common, followed by *t* and *a*. *Q*, *z*, and *x* are the most uncommon, and so on.

By the sixteenth century, another more complex system had been invented—polyalphabetic substitution. The invention was by Blaise Vigenere in 1586, although the Vigenere cipher did not come into widespread use until the nineteenth century. Consider a matrix with twenty-six different sequences of letters:

A B C D ... Z

B C D E ... A

C D E F ... B

And so on.

Then imagine a key word known only to Hans and Fritz. Let's say that the key word is "CENT," and the message is "beware." The key is repeated below the plaintext message. It says for first letter, *b*, one should go to the C row in the matrix—that would be cipher letter *d*; for second letter in plaintext, *e*, one should go to the E row in the matrix, which would be *i*, and so on.

This system is far more difficult to break than the monoalphabetic cipher—but as was shown in the nineteenth century not impossible. A shadow of the frequency vulnerability of the monoalphabetic cipher remains, and the repetition of the key word also creates a vulnerability.

The Enigma

However, in the 1920s, secrecy became mechanized, and one mechanical system looked to be invulnerable. In 1918 a German engineer, Arthur Scherbius, invented an encryption system he termed Enigma. Scherbius believed his machine would be valuable to businesses, and that is where he sought to market the machine. Alas, for Scherbius, Enigma did not catch on commercially. However, the German military came to believe that the Enigma was impregnable, and by 1925, they were incorporating it into all their services.

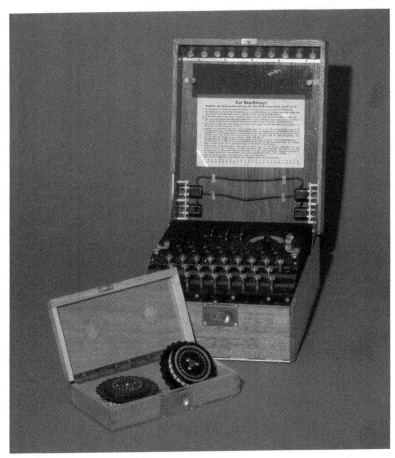

Fig. 3.1 An Enigma Machine (Courtesy of Imperial War Museum)

In essence, the Enigma machine, about the size of a desk computer, works as follows. The sender of a message types in the first plaintext letter, and a current goes to a so-called plugboard that swaps some pairs of letters—say A and U, V and R, and so on. The first plaintext letter or its swapped twin then goes to the scramblers.

The scrambler is a rotor of twenty-six letters that could be set in one of twenty-six positions. Once a plaintext letter is typed in, an electrical impulse goes to a second scrambler, and the first rotor turns one notch. After the first scrambler turns twenty-six times, the second scrambler then turns one notch. And so on to a third or fourth scrambler. A current then goes from the scrambler ensemble to a "reflector," a disk that has contacts only on its right side; it reflects the current back into the left-most scrambler, with the current traveling again through all the scramblers, and from there to a lamp-board that lights up a cipher letter. Thus, once a plaintext letter is typed in and a cipher letter is lighted on the lamp-board, the scrambler ensemble has rotated such that the next time the same plaintext letter is typed in, it lights up another, different cipher letter.

The reflector is wired such that it ensures that no letter could ever be enciphered by itself. More important, it allows the message receiver to recover the plaintext by typing in the cipher text, as long as the settings of the scramblers and plugboards are exactly the same as for the sender. Thus, if the first letter of plain text is *a*, and it creates cipher letter D, then when the receiver types in D, the plaintext letter *a* will light up.

There is one other element, so far skipped over. On the outside of each scrambler, there is a movable ring, which sets where each scrambler to its left would advance one notch. The ring, marked by letters, A to Z, could be rotated independently of the scrambler inside—thus a setting could be denoted as A-A-A. This injects still more possibilities that a code breaker will have to contend with.

The key then to be shared by the sender and receiver will be the plugboard settings (which pairs of letters are swapped), the ring setting, the order in which the scramblers are placed, and the orientation of each of the scramblers (each in one of twenty-six possible positions). Thus, for example, a U-boat going out to sea could have a month of day codes, establishing for each day the proper settings.

The Enigma machine initially had three scramblers and a plug-board that switched six pairs of letters. A day code would then set:

Order of scramblers—say, 3-2-1 [out of six possibilities].

The setting of the scramblers: say, KJW [out of $26^3 = 17,576$ possibilities].

The plugboard switches: say, A/V, R/D, X/P, U/M, T/O, Z/B [out of 100,391,791,500 possibilities[87]].

The total possibilities: ten quadrillion.

The day code would also set the ring arrangements, but we ignore this for the present.

At the start of the war, the German Enigma operators were given two more scramblers, so that any scrambler arrangement could include any three of the five scramblers available. Thus instead of the six possibilities before, there were now sixty possibilities (5 x 4 x 3). In addition, the plugboard now switched ten pairs of letters instead of the initial six. This gives in total about $159*10^{18}$ possibilities.

One key to breaking Enigma, it turned out, was to figure out how to separate scrambler settings from the plugboard.

Breaking Enigma—The Polish Cipher Bureau

The value of reading the enemy's encrypted messages in times of war seemed evident—later, some examples of this value will be discussed—and Germany's potential enemies in the 1930s, notably Poland and Great Britain, took up the challenge of breaking Enigma.

The first great success was that of the Polish Cipher Bureau and its most brilliant member, Marian Rejewski.

The Polish advance was greatly aided by a striking intelligence betrayal. An analyst in the German cipher agency in Berlin, Hans-Thilo Schmidt, in November 1931 arranged to meet with a French intelligence agent in Belgium. At that meeting, Schmidt allowed the French to photograph two sensitive documents. However, the French cryptographers were indifferent to this intelligence coup and did nothing to follow it up—other than, critically, giving the information to the Polish cryptographers. As it turned out, the information, in combination with Rejewski's mathematical analysis, allowed the Polish Cipher Bureau to deduce the wiring of the Enigma machine.

Knowing the Enigma wiring alone would not allow decryption of messages unless one also knew the key being used—the day code. But in a remarkable feat of mathematical analysis, Rejewski and his colleagues were able to figure out a way to learn the day code once they had in hand several messages.

The opening that Rejewski needed was provided by the German decision to precede every message by a three-digit code instructing the receiver how to set the scramblers before deciphering the message. The plugboard settings and the order of the scramblers would stay the same throughout the day. The three-digit code was sent using the day code for that day, and for extra assurance that the code was properly sent, the three-digit code was repeated. The Germans believed that by changing the scrambler settings for each message, they would greatly increase the security of Enigma, but in this they were badly mistaken.

For example, let us say that for the first message, the receiver is instructed to set the scrambler setting as K J H. The sender sends out the plaintext message K J H K J H. Given the day code, the message would come out as say A D F X V P. So even though Rejewski had no idea what the day code was, he did know that the first and fourth letters are related, and second and fifth, and third and sixth. That is, the day code codes the K as A, and after the scrambler rotates three times, then codes the K as X. Similarly with J being ciphered as D and V, and so on. So we have combination of (A/X), (D/V), (F/P). And this could be done for other messages, all with a new plaintext three-digit number repeating but coded by the same day code.

Rejewski then focused on loops. The following discussion is based on Simon Singh, *The Code Book*.[88] Consider for example a series of messages, all in the same day code, that give the relations of the first and fourth letter: say A/X, X/G, G/V, and then V/A. This is a loop, A back to A, a chain with four links. Then for each letter, A to Z, the number of links could be calculated. So with one particular day code, there might be three chains of four letters each, one chain of six, and one chain of eight—the letters always adding up to twenty-six of course. Similarly, loops could be found for the second and fifth letters and third and sixth letter of the repeated codes sent with each message. Each day code would then have a characteristic array of chains and links, based on looking at the first and fourth, the second and fifth, and the third and sixth letters of the message codes. A great insight of Rejewski was that the chain-link array depends only on the scrambler settings—not on the plugboard. Simon Singh, in his impressive *The Code Book*, shows this clearly:

First letter: A B C D E F G H I J K L M N O P Q R S T U V W X Y Z
Fourth letter: F Q H P L W O G B M V R X U Y C Z I T N J E A S D K

This gives four chains of three links, nine links, seven links, and seven links:

A>F>W>A
B>Q>Z>K>V>E>L>R>I>B
C>H>G>O>Y>D>P>C
J>M>X>S>T>N>U>J

Say that the plugboard was set for the above at a swap of S and G, and that instead now it is T and K that are swapped.

The chain-link array would then be:

A>F>W>A
B>Q>Z>T>V>E>L>R>I>B
C>H>S>O>Y>D>P>C
J>M>X>G>K>N>U>J

Again it would be four chains of three links, nine links, seven links, and seven links as before.

This result is that the chain-link array does not depend upon the plugboard settings and reduces the number of settings to be tested from over a quadrillion to "only" 105,456.

The Enigma wiring deduced by Rejewski was critical in that it allowed Rejewski and colleagues to try out all the scrambler settings and catalog what chain-link arrays they produced. This took about one year. Then when he had the chains for the new day code, which would require looking at about eighty messages, he could check with his catalog to see what matched.

Once the scrambler settings were found, the decryption would still have to depend on determining the plugboard switches. This was done by printing out thousands of words using the correct scrambler arrangement and then looking for words such as "rettew," which suggests the plaintext word "wetter" [weather] with the r and w swapped and e and t not swapped.

However, in late 1938, the Germans suddenly changed their indicator method. Instead of sending a scrambler setting for each message encoded by the day-code setting, they now preceded each message by a three-letter setting (sent in the open) followed by the twice-enciphered message setting indicator. The wheel order, plugboard, and ring setting were still specified for each day. The change made it impossible for the Polish Cipher Bureau to collect the eighty or so messages needed to establish the chain-link characteristic to be compared with the catalog. Although the initial three-letter setting of the scramblers is sent in the open, without the other information in the day code, the code breakers would be at a loss on how to decrypt the message.[89]

Despite this setback, Rejewski and colleagues soon invented another way to reconstruct the day code. Their method (described in some detail in *Battle of Wits* but will not be here) involved laborious trial and error, which the Poles then mechanized by the construction of machines that could quickly run through thousands of different settings. They termed these machines *bomba*; with six running in parallel, they could check out all the possible orderings of the three scramblers.[90]

The Polish Cipher Bureau's feat of decryption is only touched on in the above. It involved much more analysis, and in the words of Simon Singh, the simplified summary should not mislead one "into underestimating Rejewski's extraordinary achievement."[91]

Throughout the 1930s, the Polish Cipher Bureau was able to read the German radio traffic on a daily basis. However, in 1938, as mentioned above, the Germans increased the complexity of Enigma by having five scramblers from which three would be chosen to be emplaced on any given day. In January 1939, they further complicated matters by increasing the plugboard switches from six to ten pairs. Also, not long thereafter (in May 1940), the Germans stopped the three-letter indicator code to start each message. The 1938–39 changes effectively ended the Polish ability to decipher Enigma. The challenge for doing so shifted to the British Government Code and Cipher School (GC&CS), the focus of British code breaking after World War I, which had newly established itself in Bletchley Park, located about forty miles northwest of London.[92]

Breaking Enigma—Bletchley Park

At the center of Bletchley Park was a rambling old Victorian-Tudor mansion, soon to be supplemented by a series of wooden huts, in which various specific code-breaking activities would be focused.

For example, Hut 6 attacked the German Army Enigma communications, Hut 3 operatives translated the messages from Hut 6 and sought to exploit the information; Hut 8 specialized in the Navy Enigma, who passed their decrypts to Hut 4. Initially Bletchley had a staff of two hundred, but by the end of the war, it housed seven thousand men and women.[93]

With war looming, on July 24, 1939, members of the Polish Cipher Bureau met with members of French and British intelligence in Warsaw and unveiled there, to the astonishment of their interlocutors, two Enigma replicas and blueprints for the Polish bomba, and revealed the techniques the Poles had developed to attack Enigma. This was just in time—five weeks later, Germany invaded Poland, starting World War II.[94] The key members of the Polish Cipher Bureau, including Rejewski, still in Warsaw at the outset of the war, escaped first to Romania, then to France, and eventually to England. For reasons that are unclear, the Polish cryptographers never themselves came to Bletchley Park.[95]

One invaluable lesson the British learned from the Polish experience was the value of mathematicians in code breaking, and at Bletchley, in the fall of 1939, four outstanding young mathematicians joined the staff, supplementing the classic scholars, linguists, and others who had traditionally been the principal cryptographers in Great Britain. The most brilliant was Alan Turing, twenty-seven years old in 1939, and already author of path-breaking papers in mathematics. Turing, having done his PhD work at Princeton University (awarded the PhD in 1938) and been a visiting fellow at the Princeton Institute of Advanced Study, was a Fellow at Kings College, Cambridge University at the time he began part-time work with GC&C in September 1938. He joined Bletchley Park full-time on September 4, 1939, three days after the start of World War II. Within two months, he had revolutionized the attack on Enigma and set the stage for all Enigma decryption during the war.

One of Turing's seminal papers was "On Computable Numbers," published in 1937. This paper examined a highly theoretical question, formulated by the mathematician Kurt Godel, of what theorems in mathematics are decidable and which not. In tackling the question, Turing invented what he called a universal Turing machine, which would work as follows in the words of Stephen Budiansky:

> His conceptual machine would scan a strip of paper tape that was divided into a series of squares and detect whether the square it was looking at had a mark on it or not. This machine ... could then be programmed to perform a sequence of just four different operations: it could move the tape one square to the left or one square to the right; it could place a mark on the square or erase the mark. Turing's remarkable mathematical discovery was that any calculation that was calculable at all could be solved by such a machine. So powerful was Turing's insight that this concept would later become the foundation of the logical operations used in all digital electronic computers.[96]

Turing's capacity to imagine such a virtual machine was paralleled by a knack of imagining and then actually building real machines. As described below, this rare capacity both for deep mathematical analysis and practical machine building was critical to Turing's attack on Enigma. While working at Bletchley, Turing, a talented long-distance runner, occasionally ran the forty miles (65 km) to London when he was needed for high-level meetings, and he was capable of world-class marathon standards.[97]

Turing and Bletchley, from the onset, sought to develop an attack strategy that did not depend upon the Germans using the double encipher indicator at the start of each message, given the prospect that the Germans could end that procedure at any moment. And, in fact as noted, in the summer of 1940, they did end it.

Turing's approach was to take advantage of cribs. How this was done is simplified below. Fuller discussions are found in *Battle of Wits, Code Book,* and *Enigma.* Cribs are guesses on what the plaintext was for some string of cipher text. For example, in early morning messages describing the weather conditions in the North Atlantic, some string, say SCGHJK, may be guessed to represent "wetter" in plaintext. Sometimes a crib can be guessed, but the exact parallel cipher text may not be evident immediately. The plaintext and cipher text can then be compared—with the plaintext moved along a line above the cipher text until it is seen that no letter of plaintext is coded by same letter in the cipher text—a coding that Enigma does not allow.

Using cribs, Turing and colleagues took advantage of a weakness in Enigma, not realized by the Germans. This is that with the scrambler in the first (right-hand) position, a short crib would be unlikely to trigger a turnover of the middle rotor. Thus, the effect of the reflector and the left and middle rotors could be taken as a constant.[98] This gave a kind of backdoor attack on Enigma. The first attack, organized by Turing, used another kind of loop analysis.[99] Say "wetter" goes to "ETJWBT" is guessed crib. Then first scrambler setup S gives *w* to E, S+1 gives *e* to T, and S+3 gives *t* to W. This is a loop. Turing then designed a machine setup that would seek to reconstruct this loop for some scrambler setting.

The machine setup would work like this. The first machine, set at some three-letter orientation, would try to encipher *w* into E; the second machine set at the same setting, but moved forward one place, *e* to T; and the third, with same setting, moved forward three places *t* to W. The three machines were wired together electrically to perform a chain of logical deductions based on the crib, in such a way that if the orientation setting is not the correct one (that is, the one used in the day code), a light would indicate that a contradiction had occurred and rule out that setting, moving on to the next. Most of the possible settings would cause contradictions and be discarded, leaving only a few to be investigated in detail. The first machines were installed in March 1940.

Gordon Welchman, another Cambridge mathematician who joined Bletchley at same time as Turing, realized that the Turing design did not exploit the Enigma weakness to the full, and he invented a piece of electrical circuitry (to be called the "diagonal board") to attach to the Turing machine, which allowed a tremendous improvement in the machine design, and in particular did not require that the crib sequence contain a loop.[100]

The genius of the Turing and Welchman strategy is that the number of possibilities to be gone through by the machines does not depend upon the plugboard settings. So, just as was done in the Polish strategy of attack, the problem is reduced a hundred-billion-fold. All the scrambler settings, including the order in which the scramblers are placed, would have to be gone through by the machines, but without the vast multiplication of possibilities introduced by the plugboard, the effort was manageable.

The resulting machines employing the Turing and Welchman innovations were called bombes, using the same term as the Poles did for their machines. They were four meters by four meters by two meters and capable of working through a half a million rotor positions in hours. Their rapid construction once Turing and colleagues had presented the bombe blueprint was an impressive engineering achievement.[101] The bombes were generally operated by members of the Women's Royal Naval Service (Wrens), young women who also served at Bletchley as wireless operators and in many other functions. By the end of the war, their numbers grew from hundreds to thousands, which naturally enough led to many Bletchley romances.[102]

Once the day-code setting of the scramblers was determined,

the plugboard swaps could generally quickly be found by locating words, such as "tewwer" as described above for the Polish decryption.

Fig. 3.2. A Bletchley Bombe—Critical in the Decoding of the German Enigma (Courtesy of Sarah Hartwell)

In the words of Simon Singh, "The combination of crib, loops, and electrically connected machines resulted in a remarkable piece of cryptanalysis, and only Turing with his unique background in mathematical machines could ever have come up with it."[103]

The Dilemma of Shark

As already indicated, there was not just one kind of Enigma. In fact, all the German services had their own versions, many of them depending on the theater of operation—the Luftwaffe versions were given the names of insects (Hornet, Wasp, Cockroach), the army were given the names of birds (Phoenix, Vulture, and other); the navy were given the names of fish (Dolphin for the home water key used in the Atlantic and Baltic, and Shark for the Atlantic U-boats).[104] Overall, the U-boat Enigma was the version hardest to break, especially after January 1942.

In that month, the Germans introduced a new version of Shark, the U-boat key for the Atlantic. The changes now gave Enigma operators a choice of eight scramblers, four of which would be emplaced. Bletchley did not yet have bombes that could tackle the new version.

There was some hope that Bletchley could use short weather signals as cribs in tackling the new Shark, but in January 1942, the Germans put a new weather short signal book into effect. As a result, Bletchley was blacked out of Shark traffic for much of 1942.

The breakthrough came in October 1942, when U-boat U-599 was forced to the surface in the Mediterranean by four destroyers that had converged on it. As the boat was on the verge of sinking, three British crew from one of the destroyers, Lieutenant Anthony Fasson, Sea-man Colin Grazier, and Tommy Brown, a sixteen-year-old canteen assistant, courageously swam over to the sub and went down to the communications room, retrieving the complete indicator list and code tables for the new weather short signals. With the boat taking on water, Brown, who had already made three trips, was told not to go down again, and Fasson and Grazier to come up immediately. The two did not make it and went down with the boat—they were posthumously awarded the Georgia Cross for acts of gallantry by civilians.[105] Brown was awarded the lesser George medal and then discharged for being underage. The code tables were sent to Bletchley Park, where they provided the critical cribs needed to break the new Shark.[106]

Ultra and Its Successes

The decrypts emerging from Bletchley Park were termed "Ultra," and the British and later the Americans as well went to great lengths to protect the secret that Enigma was broken. This was done by severely limiting the number of people who would have access to Ultra and also contriving, when Ultra was used to guide action, to make the Germans think there were other ways that the information could have been obtained. For example, when Ultra was able to help in locating U-boat wolf packs, the British, where possible, sent out patrol planes, which they hoped the Germans would think were the means by which the British discovered the whereabouts of the U-boats.

During the Battle of Britain, Ultra decrypts allowed the British to understand better what the Luftwaffe was planning. For instance, they were forewarned through Ultra of the Luftwaffe's massive attacks on Eagle Day and after. On September 17, British intelligence intercepted a secret radio message, which Bletchley Park deciphered, that Hitler officially decided to postpone operation Sea-Lion (invasion of Britain).[107]

In 1941, in one critical theater of operation, Ultra dramatically failed to alter the course of the war. Ultra decrypts confirmed to the British that Germany was about to launch an invasion of the Soviet Union, and this information was conveyed to the Soviets (though not its provenance). But Stalin steadfastly refused to believe this and indeed believed that it was a British ruse to get the Soviets and Germany into a war.[108]

Ultra contributed vitally in the battle of North Africa. Between July and October 1942, while Rommel's army was battling with the British, the British effectively cut off fuel and ammunition supplies reaching Rommel by targeting ships crossing the Mediterranean. During that period, they sank forty-seven supply ships, totaling 169,000 tons. In forty-four of these cases, the ship's time of sailing, route, or location in port was relayed by Bletchley Park to the British Navy and RAF commands in Cairo. Much of the decryption came from insecure Italian messages, but these were supplemented by Ultra readings of German Enigma, which greatly added to the precision by which Britain was able to locate supply ships. Starved for fuel, Rommel was fatally weakened.[109]

In the Battle of the Atlantic, discussed more fully in the next chapter, Ultra also played a critical role. Before being blacked out by Shark in 1942, Ultra decrypts were valuable in allowing the Allies to divert convoys away from waiting U-boat wolf packs. But they became especially valuable after Shark was finally broken at the end of 1942. One result was that Ultra discovered in the spring of 1943 that the Germans were reading UK naval cipher number 3. The British then developed naval cipher number 5, which came into full use in June, blinding the Germans until the end of the war.

In another later development, by mid-1943, Ultra was also able to locate the rendezvous spots where the German submarine fuel tankers were sent—these were the so-called milk cows critical to extending the ranges of the U-boats. At first, the British were adamant not to attack, in fear that doing so would give away that Shark had been broken. But the increased deployment of aircraft carriers and patrol planes made it more plausible that the Germans would think that the boats had been spotted by aircraft even when in fact it was Ultra that did so, and so the risk of compromising Ultra waned. After May 1943, the milk cows were attacked with devastating effect. By July 1944, sixteen of the seventeen tanker U-boats that had been built were sunk. As the tide turned against the U-boats in the spring of 1943, Ultra was also valuable in revealing a sharp erosion of morale among the submarine crews.

Doenitz, the commander of the U-boats, became suspicious in 1943 and 1944 that German ciphers had been broken but was assured that was not so. He generally blamed the increased Allied identification of sub locations on radar, Allied patrol planes, high-frequency direction finding (HF-DF), and a suspicion that the Allies were somehow using infrared detection to locate submarines. The latter suspicion was discovered by Ultra, which led the British to immediately further fan the suspicions through the use of double agents.[110]

Ultra played a critical role in the great deception campaigns that the Allies launched during the war—notably before the landings in North Africa in 1942, in Sicily in 1943, and D-Day in June 1944. In this endeavor, Ultra was valuable in two ways. First, it allowed the Allies to understand better what the preconceived notions of the Germans were—which the intelligence services could then use to fortify what the Germans already believed. Second, and crucially,

Ultra was able to allow the Allies to continually monitor what the Germans believed from the deception campaign.

Whether Ultra markedly shortened the war, as many contend, is probably unprovable, but it, without question, contributed significantly in many of the key battles of the war. To know what your enemy is thinking and planning is priceless, and Ultra, in this sense, has to be considered one of the greatest achievements of the war.

Given so, it is sad that the folks at Bletchley Park did not get credit for what they had done until almost thirty years after the war ended—Bletchley had been kept secret by the Allies until 1974 and all participants sworn to uphold this secrecy. The reasons for this are somewhat murky, though in part it was apparently due to the fact that the British had sent Enigma machines to many countries for their use in encryption and did not want the recipients to know that the Enigma had been broken. Whatever the reasons, the thirty-year delay meant that many of the key people at Bletchley died before their significant contributions were made known.

The most tragic of these code breakers was Alan Turing. In 1952, he naively admitted to a homosexual encounter, which led to him being arrested on the charge of indecency under the Criminal Law Amendment of 1885. He was forced to see a psychiatrist and to undergo hormone treatment. Sinking into depression, in 1954 Turing killed himself by biting an apple laced with cyanide—recalling a line from the Wicked Witch in *Snow White*, which Turing knew well: "Dip the apple in the brew, let the sleeping death seep through."[111]

Postscript: Code Breaking Other Than Enigma

Of course, all the principal belligerents in World War II—not just the Germans—encrypted their radio communications, and, to a greater or lesser extent, all sought to decipher their adversaries' communications. Japan's sophisticated encryption systems proved especially daunting to American cryptographers, and the successful breaking of the principal Japanese diplomatic and naval codes by the Americans marked achievements as impressive in many ways as the breaking of Enigma. The chief Japanese diplomatic code, termed the purple code (like Enigma, a machine-generated code), was broken before Pearl Harbor. The still more complex Japanese JN-25 naval code was broken during the months after Pearl Harbor. The information garnered from the code breaking was given the name "Magic" in parallel with the "Ultra" derived from the breaking of Enigma. The character of the Japanese codes and how they were broken are not discussed here, but the interested reader may consult several excellent sources noted in the bibliography.

One of the first and most dramatic contributions of Magic was the deciphering by the United States of Japanese naval code messages in the spring of 1942, in the months after Pearl Harbor. These messages made evident that the Japanese were intending to undertake a major invasion of some American target in June 1942. The target was referred to in the communications as "AF." The American analysts were reasonably sure that AF stood for the island of Midway, a small but vital atoll in the Pacific about 1,300 miles west of Hawaii. To confirm this, the Americans instructed the military at Midway to send a radio message in the clear back to the States, stating that the desalination plant at Midway was having problems. The Americans then soon intercepted and decoded Japanese messages that AF was experiencing desalination problems. With Magic providing then the date of the Japanese attack, the place of the attack, and much about the nature of the Japanese fleet headed toward Midway, the US naval commanders were able to alert the Midway military base there and to send three aircraft carriers to a position near Midway best able to respond to the approaching Japanese fleet. In the resulting battle, the Americans sank four Japanese carriers and killed many of Japan's most experienced naval pilots. After the war, the Japanese naval officers interrogated all deemed this battle the critical turning point of the war in the Pacific.

With respect to decoding efforts by the Axis powers, the German navy's code-breaking bureau, called B-Dienst for short, was very active and resourceful. Indeed, as mentioned above, in the Battle of the Atlantic, pitting Allied convoys against German U-boats, for a period the Germans held the intelligence advantage of having broken British naval cipher number 3 while the Shark Enigma had blacked out Bletchley Park. However, as earlier noted, after the summer of 1943, the British changed their naval code and blinded German cryptographers until the end of the war.

On the Allied encoding efforts, one unusual scheme perhaps deserves special mention—the use by the US Marines of native Navajo speakers in the Pacific campaigns. Several hundred Navajos were enlisted to transmit messages over telephone or radio using codes built upon their native language. Few outside of the Navajos knew the language, and the speed of communication allowed by the Navajo speakers was striking and by all accounts highly successful.*[112]

Bibliography

Beevor, Antony. *The Second World War*. Back Bay Books, 2012.

Brown, Anthony Cave. *Bodyguard of Lies*. Quill/Willaim Morrow, 1975.

Budiansky, Stephen. *Battle of Wits: The Complete Story of Codebreaking in World War II*. Free Press, 2002.

Deighton, Len. *Fighter*. Castle Books, 2000.

Hodges, Andrew. *Alan Turing: The Enigma*. Princeton University Press, 1983, 2014.

McKay, Sinclair. *The Secret Lives of Codebreakers*. Plume, 2012.

Singh, Simon. *The Code Book: The Secret History of Codes and Code-Breaking*, Fourth Estate, 2000

---

* Other Native American code talkers were also used in the war, including Lakota soldiers, though not on the scope of the Navajos.

CHAPTER 4

⚛️

The Battle of the Atlantic

The U-Boat Threat

The Battle of the Atlantic was not one limited to a single period of time. It was waged over the entire war, and most dramatically and critically from 1941 to 1943. It ranged German U-boats (attack submarines) against Allied shipping of vital materials and food from North American ports to Great Britain and the Soviet Union. To the Germans, if they could deny enough supplies getting to Britain, they could starve the British into defeat. To Churchill, "The only thing that really frightened me during the war was the U-boat threat."[113]

In 1941, the U-boats took a toll on shipping to Britain, but the damage was limited by German reluctance to attack US ships, lest that would bring the United States into the war. Once the United States entered the war, however, the U-boats were unleashed, and the losses of Allied ships and tonnage rose dramatically. In early 1942, the United States disdained convoys and sailed ships alone—with devastating results. Matters changed rapidly, however, and by the spring of 1942, the United States was shipping materials to the Allies largely in convoys. In general, it was found that the number of ships sunk in a U-boat attack was independent of the size of the convoy—thus the bigger the convoy the better. Also the number of escorts to guard a convoy is proportional to the perimeter of the area surrounding the ships, while the number of ships is roughly proportional to the area—again an argument for large convoys. The escorts during much of the battle were destroyers and smaller corvettes armed with depth charges.

Some convoys were "fast"—over nine knots; some were slow—about seven knots.* Convoy sizes ranged from twenty to sixty ships during the year. The convoys were designated by ports of origin and destination and by whether fast or slow: "HX" designated fast convoys to the UK out of Halifax or sometimes New York; "SC" designated slow convoys from New York to the UK; "ON" designated convoys (without cargo) returning westward, UK to New York.

The bulk of the U-boats were type VII, weighing approximately 750 tons, with a maximum speed of seventeen knots, a radius of operation of eight thousand miles, and an armament of eleven torpedoes. In 1942, the fleet was supplemented by type IX boats of 1,100 tons and a cruising range of over thirteen thousand miles and an armament of twenty-two torpedoes.[114] The living conditions were brutal—one toilet for forty-four men that could not be used when the boat was submerged, no air-conditioning, no showers, precious little food or even fresh air much of the time.[115]

During 1942, much went against the Allies. In February 1942, the Germans added a fourth rotor to their Enigma machine, creating the so-called Shark variant of Enigma, and Bletchley Park was blacked out for nine months. It was then possible for the Germans to direct submarines into the path of incoming convoys and difficult for the Allies to know exactly where the wolf packs lay in wait.[116] Air patrols near the US and British coasts kept the U-boats at bay in these areas, but there remained a roughly six-hundred-mile gap in

---

* One knot = one nautical mile per hour. A nautical mile is defined as one minute of arc measured along any meridian. By international convention, it is 1,852 meters; it is about 1.15 times a standard mile.

the North Atlantic where the Allies did not have air cover; this is where the German U-boat threat was greatest. Although the Allies had some airborne radar, the Germans in the fall of 1942 developed a receiver set, "Metox," which gave warning of aircraft approaching using the 1.7-meter wavelength of the airborne radar.[117]

The Allies had two, partially conflicting, strategic goals—one to guard the sheep, that is to have convoys avoid the U-boat wolf packs if they could; and two, to attack the wolves. During much of 1942, guarding the sheep was the dominant goal. Even without cryptographic intelligence (with the Shark blackout) for part of this period, the Allies were able to some extent to locate where the wolf packs were operating. Between May 1942 and May 1943, "105 out of 174 convoys sailed across the Atlantic without interference from submarines; and out of the 69 sighted by the wolf packs 23 escaped without attack and 30 suffered only minor losses."[118]

Nevertheless, in 1942, total losses in the Atlantic reached 7.8 million tons, 5.4 million tons due to U-boats, much of the rest due to aircraft attacks. British imports had sunk to one-third of their peacetime level. By January 1943, the British navy had only two months' supply of oil left.[119] German U-boat losses in 1942 were eighty-four, more than made up by new construction. By the beginning of 1943, the Germans had 240 submarines in operation— though not all of them deployed in the Atlantic at any one time.

Between January and May 1943, the Battle of the Atlantic reached its crisis.[120] The winter of 1942–43 was harsh, and the roiling seas of the Atlantic limited both U-boat losses and the losses to U-boats. The weather cleared by March. Just at the end of another blackout of Shark, though this time for only ten days, two large convoys, HX-229 and SC-122, converged on each other and came under withering attacks by the German wolf packs. Twenty-one ships were sunk. Overall, in March the shipping losses were devastating—over six hundred thousand tons sunk, at the cost to the Germans of fifteen submarines.[121]

But this turned out to be the high-water mark for the U-boat threat.

In the next months, there was a startling and dramatic reversal of fortune, so dramatic that in late May 1943, the Germans temporarily withdrew most of their U-boats from the North Atlantic. On May 23, Admiral Doenitz, the commander of the submarines, ordered a "temporary shifting of operations to areas less endangered by aircraft."[122]

Counterattack—Closing the Air Gap and Ultra

Despite the March losses, already by late 1942, the tide was turning in the Allies' favor. First of all, a person of tremendous abilities, Sir Admiral Max Horton, assumed leadership of the Allied effort. Horton kept unusual hours. He worked in the morning, then took off each day for a leisurely round of golf between 2:00 and 6:00 p.m., and then went off to work again until well after midnight. Horton immediately agitated for more air cover and for more convoy escorts, and he insisted on far more extensive training of escorts— improving their tactics and coordination in attacking the U-boats. Also, as confidence in tactics increased, Horton more and more turned to a strategy of attacking the wolves, no longer seeking to avoid confrontation with the U-boats.[123]

Secondly and critically, the Atlantic air gap gradually was closing. Some long-range bombers equipped with fuel drop tanks to markedly increase their range were diverted from other missions to the Battle of the Atlantic, and the first American escort aircraft carriers to accompany the convoys began appearing in March 1943.[124]

Thirdly, the German Shark Enigma was finally broken in December 1942, as described in the preceding chapter, with Ultra thus playing a critical role in the battle against the German U-boats.

Science in the Turning of the Tide

Lastly and decisively, several technical developments came into play to supplement older technologies such as depth charges and sonar detection of underwater objects. These included a new means of destruction—the hedgehog weapon to supplement the depth charge, and three new means of detection—Leigh lights, high-frequency direction finding (HF/DF), and most dramatically, microwave (centimetric) radar, increasingly deployed on escort vessels and patrol aircraft.

Hedgehog

The Hedgehog was a multi-headed launcher that fired twenty-four grenades forward of the warship. It had several advantages over the depth charge. Unlike the depth charge, which was an explosive set to detonate at some preprogrammed depth, the Hedgehog grenade exploded on contact, and, moreover, it did not distort sonar readings.

By the end of the war, Hedgehogs had destroyed close to fifty enemy submarines. Its more sophisticated replacements, the Squid and the Limbo weapons systems (which could go deeper and actually search for the submarine), added a dozen or more to that total.[125]

Fig. 4.1 The Hedgehog: A Multiheaded Launcher That Fired Twenty-Four Grenades Forward of the Warship (Courtesy of Imperial War Museum)

Leigh Lights

Since 1941, the Allies had been sending air patrols over the Bay of Biscay. This is the three-hundred-mile by three-hundred-mile area that the U-boats had to transit from their ports in France to get to the convoy lanes. This was dangerous for the U-boats, and they had resorted to transiting the bay underwater during the day, and above surface at night, when they could go much faster. Airborne radar could detect the boats at night, but partly because of strong returns from the sea, it did not work well when the planes came close to the subs—within about one mile.

But in early 1942, an RAF officer at Coastal Command headquarters, Squadron Leader Humphrey De Verd Leigh, came up with an invention to bridge the gap between the minimum radar range and the point of attack. This was a searchlight attached to the patrol planes based on a carbon arc lamp that would need only seven 12-volt batteries. The whole apparatus weighed less than 600 pounds.[126]

By June 1942, the first Leigh Lights were operating and the number of nighttime attacks increased sharply. However, in later 1942, the Germans countered by deploying a receiver that could detect the signals from the British 1.7 m airborne radars, the so-called Metox system. This would allow the U-boat to submerge before the planes could attack. The Allied counter-counter move came later, as discussed below, when the planes deployed the 10-cm radar, which the Germans could not detect.

HF-DF

Next to code breaking and radar, HF/DF (known as "huff-duff" to the sailors) was probably the most dangerous Allied technology facing the U-boats. Its goal was to locate the U-boats through detection of radio communications from U-boats to one another or to shore stations. In this, it struck at the heart of wolf-pack tactics, namely the communications needed to gather the group into position to attack convoys. Had the U-boats operated under more strict radio silence, the wolf packs would have been a lot harder to form. The radio signals transmitted by the subs were short—on the order of twenty seconds—so that it was critical that the huff-duff system could locate the source of a signal almost instantly.

The technology was not completely new, as it had been used to find bearings on medium and low frequencies for navigation purposes for years. The Royal Navy, however, was the first to design an apparatus that could take bearings on the high-frequency radio transmitters employed by the German U-boats—3–30 MHz—and to do this rapidly. The system used so successfully in the war was developed by a small group of scientists at the Admiralty Signals Establishment.[127]

The basic elements of huff-duff were arrangements of two loop aerials at right angles to each other that allowed the direction of the detected radio wave to be determined. Range could be found through triangulation if more than one huff-duff set detected the signal, or, at short range, by measuring the strength of the signal.[128]

At first, the huff-duff system consisted of a number of shore stations in the British Isles, Iceland, Greenland, and Bermuda. Later it became possible to outfit escort ships with huff-duff on a high mast. When the U-boats were detected, it became possible to instruct convoys to evade the U-boats, or later in the war, when antisubmarine tactics and capabilities improved, to attack the U-boats. In intercepting the U-boat radio communication, it was not necessary to understand what the U-boat was saying, which was, of course, encrypted. At the height of its effectiveness, huff-duff was able to locate U-boats on the surface up to sixty-five kilometers away.[129]

Analysts estimate that huff-duff contributed to one-quarter of all U-boats sunk during the war. Failing to implement a severe radio silence after 1942 was one of the most fateful mistakes made by the German U-boat command.

Fig. 4.2 HF-DF, High-Frequency Direction Finding, allowed the Allies to locate U-boats by intercepting U-boat radio traffic. (Courtesy of Imperial War Museum)

Microwave Radar

Early on, the radar pioneers realized how valuable it would be to develop radars using wavelengths much shorter than the meter-length radiation employed in the Chain Home system that played such a key role in the Battle of Britain. Initially such shorter, centimeter-wavelength or microwave, radar was wanted most urgently for air defense against nighttime bomber raids, but as the Battle of the Atlantic developed, its great value in that battle also became clear. Its two greatest assets were one, that, not requiring large antennas, it could be put on airplanes and on escort ships, and two, that it could generate a narrow beam, potentially able to locate a submarine conning tower and to do so without the U-boat knowing that it had been located. Unlike Metox, which as noted was able to detect illumination by 1.7 m airborne radar, the U-boats did not have (and would never have) the means to detect the shorter-wave radar.

Remember that antenna gain is proportional to the antenna area and inversely proportional to the wavelength. One of the pioneering scientists in the early days of radar tasked with developing airborne radar, E.G. (Taffy) Bowen, a young Welshman, who had gone with Watson-Watt to work on the Chain Home system described in chapter 2, reasoned as follows:

> By far, the most limiting factor in in airborne radar at 200 Mc/s [wave length 1.5 m] was the enormous signal which came from the ground directly below the aircraft. Aircraft echoes beyond that range would simply be wiped out by the much stronger signals coming from the ground. The only way of improving the system would be to project a narrow beam forward to get rid of the ground returns. I estimated that a beam width of 10 degrees was required to achieve this. Given an aperture of 30 inches—the maximum available in the nose of a fighter—this called for an operating wavelength of 10 centimeters.[130]

The tremendous potential value of 10-cm radar was thus early realized, and Henry Tizard, chairman of the Aeronautical Research Committee, and as discussed in chapter 2, one of the key persons behind the Chain Home radar network, funded research to achieve it. One problem was that there did not seem to exist an oscillator that could generate the needed power. To seek a means of generating such power was one of the critical goals of the research.

At the University of Birmingham, Physics Department, one of the places undertaking research on radar, under the direction of Marcus Oliphant, two young physicists, John Randall and Henry Boot, were put to work. In 1939, Randall, then thirty-five years old, had the previous summer gone to Wales on vacation with his wife and son and came across an English translation of Heinrich Hertz's *Electric Waves*, where Hertz described his spark gap experiment. In this experiment, Hertz's receiver consisted of a loop of wire with a small gap across the two ends across which a spark jumped and generated an electromagnetic wave. Randall wondered whether Hertz's loop could be extended to three dimensions, and instead of a loop of wire, there would be a cylinder with a slit; and he then considered how this could be used in an oscillator. He then imagined an oscillator with several cylindrical cavities.[131] Hertz found that the wavelengths generated were 7.94 times the loop diameter. And Randall, working with Boot, a twenty-three-year-old graduate student, assumed that the same ratio would hold in three dimensions, so that to generate a wave of 10 cm would require a cavity of diameter about 1.4 cm. With this insight, Randall and Boot constructed a crude oscillator, later termed a cavity magnetron.[132]

The essential elements of the cavity magnetron are a cylindrical cathode emitting electrons, an anode structure that possesses cavities, an external magnetic field with flux lines parallel to the axis of the cathode, and a waveguide to withdraw the output power. The electrons emerging from the cathode are bent by the magnetic field on their way to the anode and flow over the cavities generating resonant frequencies.[133] The magnetron concocted by Randall and Boot and also the more sophisticated versions that followed were of a size that the magnetron could be held in the palm of a hand.

On February 21, 1940, Randall and Boot hooked up their cavity magnetron to a six-watt car lightbulb and immediately burned it out—and soon were generating amazing amounts of power. The first production models of the cavity magnetron began to come through the shop at Wembley in July 1940, and "their performance was outstanding."[134] With a magnetic field of 1,500 Gauss and a pulsed anode potential of ten thousand volts, they gave an output of ten kilowatts, with a distinct possibility of more to come. More sophisticated versions of the magnetron were soon produced—and it became clear that the new device had overnight dramatically increased the power that could be generated at 10-cm wavelength.

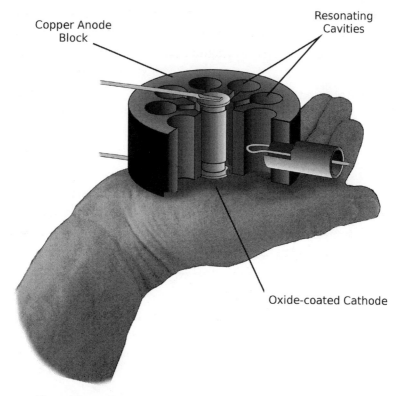

Copper Anode Block

Resonating Cavities

Oxide-coated Cathode

Fig 4.3 The cavity magnetron. This invention increased the power that could be generated of microwaves by a factor of one thousand! It became the heart of all microwave radars built during the war. (T. Daniel Feiveson)

The next step was to integrate the magnetron into operational radar sets. To support this effort, Tizard argued that the magnetron and other British technological breakthroughs should be shared with scientists in America. These included designs for rockets, gyroscopic gun-sights, superchargers, submarine detection devices, plastic explosives, self-sealing fuel tanks, and jet engines, as well as the resonant magnetron. Churchill approved this, and a small group chaired by Tizard, and including the aforementioned Taffy Bowen as the group's radar expert, was formed. In September 1940, the Tizard Mission came to the United States to explain what scientific war work the British were doing and to learn what the American scientists had been doing. The cavity magnetron was the jewel in the British presentation. On September 19 at Wardman Hotel in Washington, the mission unveiled the cavity magnetron to the astonishment of the US group there. The magnetron generated ten kilowatts of power at 10 cm, a one-thousand-fold increase to what the Americans had been able to do!

Impelled by this meeting, the United States soon formed the Radiation Laboratory at MIT founded in November 1940, which then developed microwave radars of various kinds incorporating the magnetron. Bell Labs undertook the production of the new radars and built over one million during the war. The first chronicler of American science during WWII, James Phinney Baxter III, captured the dramatic impact of the magnetron:

> When members of the Tizard mission brought [the cavity magnetron] to America in 1940, they carried the most valuable cargo ever brought to our shore.[135]

Operations Research

Along with these developments, one other contribution of scientists should be highlighted—that of operations research. This may be characterized as mathematical analyses by scientists and mathematicians based on close-working relations with military officers, in many cases involving data derived from military operations. Such collaboration of scientists and military is something the Germans never did systematically.

The British navy operations group was headed by P.M.S. Blackett, who you will remember was a member of the Tizard Committee that drove the British radar development, and incidentally a future Nobel laureate.

Some of the insights of the operations researchers may seem obvious after reflection but were not initially fully understood. For example, in 1942, the operations research staff at the British Coastal Command undertook a study of how to increase the number of flying hours of planes patrolling the waters for U-boats. Their central finding was that the RAF's serviceability goal of having 75 percent of the aircraft of each squadron ready for operational duty at all times was a mistake. So the operations researchers came up with the counterintuitive finding that by accepting a lower serviceability rate, the total number of monthly flying hours would increase. In a way, this is not so surprising. As Blackett pointed out, the reductio ad absurdum of the RAF policy of focusing on serviceability would be not to fly at all—that would lead to a serviceability rate of 100 percent! [136]

Other insights depended on careful collection of data on actual operations and construction of models, for example on determining at what depth to detonate depth charges. The lethal radius of a 450-pound depth charge was twenty-five feet, and the charges were set to be detonated at some specified depth.

The navy had been setting depth charges to detonate at one hundred feet depth. This was done based on calculations that, on average, a sub, having spotted an escort destroyer, would immediately dive and be out of sight for about fifty seconds before the escort reached the point at which the sub was last seen. Given a dive rate of about two feet per second, this would put the sub at one hundred feet depth. The problem, not realized until the operations research analysis, was that in fifty seconds the sub would not only be at a hundred-foot depth or close to that but would also be far horizontally from the point of the depth charge release. And data confirmed the problem. As of May 1941, the success rate against attacked U-boats was only about 1 percent. So taking an average time of sub escape as fifty seconds to determine optimum depth of detonation gave the worst of two possible worlds. If the sub was at one hundred feet depth, it would also have had time to travel over a wide area; if it had less time to dive, it would be within a potentially lethal area but at a much lesser depth than the charges detonated. The operations research team proposed that henceforth the depth charges be detonated at twenty-five feet and predicted that this would increase the success rate against the U-boats ten-fold or more. And so it turned out.

Reversal of Fortune[137]

By the spring of 1943, all these developments were in place—decisive leadership, greater numbers of escorts, air cover provided by long-range bombers and escort aircraft carriers, Ultra, HF/DF, centimetric radar, and other.

The reversal of fortune in the Battle of the Atlantic was sudden and decisive after the high losses of 600,000 tons in March of 1943. Thus in April 1943, the tonnage losses to U-boats were halved—to 327,000 tons at a loss of fifteen U-boats. In May 1943, tonnage losses dropped to 264,000 tons with a rise in U-boat losses to a staggering forty-one boats. Between March 1943 and December 1943, the number of merchant ships sunk decreased markedly, and the number of U-boats sunk rose dramatically. Thus, in March 1943, ninety merchant ships were sunk at a cost of twelve U-boats. But by May 1943, forty ships were sunk at a cost of almost forty U-boats. From July 1943 to the end of the year, far more U-boats were sunk than merchant ships, over one hundred U-boats.[138]

During the first week in May, Doenitz, commander of the German U-boat fleet, attacked Convoy ONS-5 and sank thirteen ships, but seven U-boats were sunk by escorts and aircraft, and five others damaged. Later in May, thirty-three U-boats attacked Convoy

SC- 130; no ships were sunk, and five U-boats were lost. One, U-954, was sunk by a Liberator (the B-24 long-range US bomber); all the crew were killed, including Doenitz's twenty-one-year-old son, Peter.

As noted, at the end of May, Doenitz at least temporarily gave up the battle and removed most of the U-boats from the North Atlantic. Though some U-boats returned to the Atlantic later, they never again seriously threatened convoys to Britain or to the Soviet Union. Between June and December 1943, only fifty-seven ships were sunk in the whole Atlantic, for the loss of 141 submarines. In the whole of 1944, Allied shipping losses were no more than 170,000 tons.[139] In the first three months of 1944, U-boats sank three merchantmen in convoy out of 3,360 ships sailing the Atlantic—at a cost of thirty-six submarines.

In 1944, U-boat losses were 248. Each submarine patrol was likely to be its last. No wonder that many Germans termed the U-boats the iron coffins. Overall in the war, the Germans built 1,162 U-boats; 785 were sunk. Twenty-eight thousand submariners were killed, nearly three-fourth of all those who served.[140]

Perhaps one more factor in the Battle of the Atlantic should be mentioned. While the Allied ships lost in the Atlantic between 1940 and 1943 were substantial, the amazing industrial production of the United States more than compensated. In the course of the war, the United States built 2,700 Liberty ships, the main cargo ship transiting the Atlantic, most of them in 1943–1945. Merchant ship losses in those years were fewer than eight hundred.

But it is also worth remembering that even before the immense output of US naval yards came to matter, scientific and tactical innovations played a critical role in turning around the Battle of the Atlantic.

Biblography

Beevor, Antony. *The Second World War*, chapter 29. Black Bay Books, 2012.

Bowen, E.G. *Radar Days,* chapters 9–11. Adam Hilger, 1987.

Buderi, Robert. *The Invention that Changed the World,* chapters 1–7. Simon and Schuster, 2006.

Budiansky, Stephen. *Battle of Wits.* Free Press 2002.

Budiansky, Stephen. *Blackett's War.* Vintage, 2013.

Dimbleby, Jonathan. *The Battle of the Atlantic: How the Allies Won the War.* Viking, 2015.

Hartcup, Guy. *The Effect of Science on the Second World War,* chapter 2. Palgrave, 2003.

Kennedy, Paul. *Engineers of Victory*, chapter 1. Random House, 2013.

Murray, Williamson, and Aland Millett. *A War to Be Won*, chapter 10. Belknap, 2000.

Overy, Richard. *Why the Allies Won*, chapter 2. Pimlico, 2006.

Phelps, Stephen. *The Tizard Mission.* Westholme, 2010.

Film:

The Cruel Sea—directed by Charles Frend (1953), based on a book by Nicholas Monsarrat on the adventures of a British escort ship.

Das Boot—directed by Wolfgang Peterson (1981) on the officers and men of a German U-boat in the North Atlantic.

CHAPTER 5

———— ⚛ ————

Strategic Bombing

Introduction

Strategic bombing played a critical role in the war, a role that is also highly controversial. By strategic bombing, we refer to attacks from the air on the enemy's cities and industry, as opposed to tactical bombing in support of military operations. (We include in this definition the attack on Britain by the German V-1 pilotless aircraft and the V-2 long-range rocket, as well as by manned bombers.) The story of this chapter is mostly of Allied bombing of Germany and of German industries located in satellite and occupied countries. By the last year of the war, the United States also bombed the Japanese homeland, with increasingly devastating effect. But our focus will be on the combined US and British bombing campaigns in Europe, where various electronic measures and countermeasures and other technical innovations were of central importance.

The Onset of Allied Strategic Bombing

At the start of the war in Europe, the most significant strategic bombing was by the Luftwaffe in the Battle of Britain, and after September 1940 in the blitz on London and other British cities.

One critical moment in the German bombing campaign was the British discovery in 1940 of a German system to improve bombing accuracy. The discovery was made by a young scientist in the Air Ministry, R.V. Jones. Jones, then twenty-eight years old, and with a legendary fondness for practical jokes,[141] pieced together several strands of evidence to conclude that the Germans were using radio-guidance systems, and in a dramatic meeting with the war cabinet in late June, convinced Churchill of the reality of the German systems.[142]

One piece of the evidence came in November 1939 when Jones received a package from Norway containing seven pages of a typewritten German text along with an English translation by the Norwegians. The package was received in Oslo a few days earlier as part of an unsigned document. It contained information on proximity fuses, torpedoes, and radio guidance of bombers. It was discovered after the war that the package was sent by Hans Ferdinand Mayer, a German physicist and electronics expert opposed to Hitler, though at the time this was unknown to the Norwegians or British. With this and other clues, Jones recognized later that three systems were being used. Two used beams from two or more stations to signal the bomb release point. The most sophisticated used just one station that sent out a signal for direction finding and an audio tone for ranging; the plane would pick up signal and retransmit the audio tone on another frequency, with the ground station determining range from the phase shift that came back. This system, code-named X-Gerat, matched perfectly the description in the Oslo Report.[143] The danger posed by the systems was that the Germans might be able to use them to undertake highly accurate night bombing of vital British targets, such as the Rolls-Royce works where the Merlin engines for Spitfires and Hurricanes were made.

It was therefore vital for the British to find ways to disrupt the radio guidance, which, with the information gathered by Jones, the British were soon able to do. This was done by sending out radio signals at the same frequencies that the Germans were receiving from their radio guidance stations to confuse the German pilots and by using various forms of jamming against the German transmitters.[144]

Though with such countermeasures, along with fighter defenses, the British were able to limit the impacts of the German bombing, the Germans still reigned triumphant on the ground in Europe. The only means Britain had to fight back against the German onslaught was to undertake their own strategic bombing of Germany and of parts of occupied Europe.

It quickly became apparent that day attacks were too costly against German fighter aircraft and antiaircraft fire. And by April 1940, Bomber Command had confined itself to night bombing. This, along with other reasons, made attacks on specific industrial targets virtually impossible, and by November 1940, Bomber Command was deliberately targeting civilians in cities, including presumably industrial workers, with the object of destroying morale and disrupting industrial production. There was widespread popular support for the argument that Hitler's Germany was so wicked that any methods, even if they were morally questionable, should be used to destroy it.[145]

After the German invasion of Russia in June 1941, British strategic bombing became still more important as, in effect, the only way the British could come to the aid of Russia. On the night of the German invasion, Churchill broadcast to the nation pledging British support for the Soviet Union against the Nazi "bloodthirsty guttersnipe." The one military pledge he made to Stalin was "to bomb Germany by day as well as night with ever-increasing measure."[146]

But confidence that the bombing was taking a toll on Germany soon took a jolt. In July 1941, Professor Lindemann, Churchill's scientific confidant, asked Bomber Command whether he might investigate bombing accuracy by analyzing photographs taken during operations. This was a project that had only become possible since the early summer. When the war broke out, the RAF had day cameras but none suitable for night photography. Research had begun on automatic night cameras, but they were not ready until 1942. In the meantime, the RAF had to make do with a simplified camera, not ideal but deemed adequate.[147]

Lindemann instructed a young economist on his staff, David Bensusan-Butt, to examine 650 photographs taken from one hundred raids between June 2 and July 25, 1941. The report was ready by August 18, 1941. The analysis showed that in general only one in five of all bomber aircraft sent on a mission reached within five miles of the assigned target ... one in ten over the Ruhr industrial area, and on moonless or hazy nights, one in fifteen.

This was startling, and Bomber Command, skeptical of the findings of the Butt Report, undertook its own study. In October 1941, it "reviewed accuracy for the three months following the Butt Report. It found that the average performance was even worse than feared; only 15 percent of aircraft bombed within five miles of the target point."[148]

Nevertheless, Bomber Command doubled down on its strategy of night bombing of cities, most markedly after the appointment in February 1942 of Sir Arthur Harris as commander in chief of Bomber Command. Harris had two important prejudices that colored his entire period as commander in chief. He held an exceptional hostility to the Germans, which led him not to shrink from killing civilians. His second conviction was that heavy bombing in urban areas was the best way to shorten the war.

In a way, the Butt Report on bombing inaccuracy had convinced even the critics that there was no option but to go for area targets—that is, cities. Harris was now openly defining success by the number of urban acres his bombers had reduced to rubble. Also, by 1942, four-engine Halifaxes and Lancasters started to come into service, allowing still greater rubble-producing bombing.[149]

Nonetheless, even while cities remained prime targets, there was every reason for the British to improve bombing accuracy to the extent possible. To this end, the British developed a series of guidance systems—termed Gee, Oboe, and H2S. For Bomber Command, Oboe and H2S became available in mid-1943.[150] The United States, for its part, put faith in something called the Norden bombsight.

The Quest for Bombing Accuracy: GEE, OBOE, H2S, the Norden Bombsight

Gee

This system consisted of three stations, one master and two slaves. The master station sent a pulse followed two milliseconds later by a double pulse. The first slave station sent a single pulse one millisecond after the master's single pulse, and the second slave sent a single pulse one millisecond after the master's double pulse. On board the plane, the display gave the difference in reception time of the pulses and relative distances of the stations. This allowed calculation of where the plane was. Unfortunately, just as the British found ways to interfere with the German radio guidance systems, the Germans soon developed ways to disrupt Gee.

Oboe

Oboe used two stations at different and well-separated locations in England to transmit a signal to a Mosquito pathfinder bomber carrying a radio transponder. Pulses could be short or long, allowing a Morse code to be sent.

As described by R.V. Jones, "[T]he idea was to fly an aircraft at a constant range from one station by sending out pulses from the ground which the aircraft would pick up and amplify and then return to the ground station. The ground station would then find the aircraft's range from the time it took the pulses to return. The path of the aircraft, if it flew at a constant range, would thus be part of a circle centered on the ground station, and this circle would have to pass near the target ..."[151]

Thus, the plane would fly at a constant range from the ground station at Trimingham. When it gets to an appropriate range from another station, Walmer, the Walmer station sends the order for bomb release. In the view of R.V. Jones, Oboe was the most precise bombing system of the whole war.[152]

One disadvantage was that the use of Oboe could give away where the aircraft was. The British addressed this problem by placing Oboe on Mosquito twin-engine bombers that acted as pathfinders for the bombing attacks. The Mosquito was made of wood and powered by two Rolls-Royce Merlin engines. It could fly at 400 mph and had a service ceiling of at least 28,000 feet. Its speed, altitude, and lack of a strong radar signal, given the wood construction, made it very difficult to intercept. Later in the war, Oboe used shorter wavelength signals, which the Germans could not detect.[153]

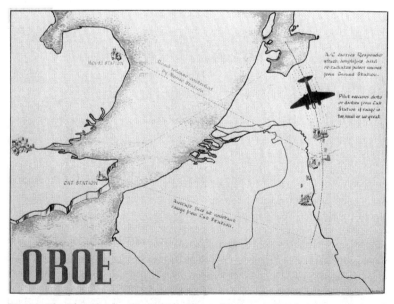

Fig. 5.1 The Oboe Bomber Navigation System (Courtesy of Imperial War Museum)

H2S

H2S was an airborne, ground-scanning radar system. It operated at 9.1 cm and then later at still lower wavelengths (higher frequencies). It allowed ground mapping for navigations. But, as discussed below, use of H2S also allowed German night fighters to hone in on the bombers, which led ultimately to a decision to shut down the H2S system on raids where large numbers of German night fighters were expected.

The Norden Bomb Sight

By the summer of 1942, the US Eighth Air Force began to assemble in Britain. Unlike the British, the Americans insisted on day bombing on specific industrial targets, a policy maintained throughout the European war.[154] One reason for this was air force confidence in its Norden Bombsight, which it claimed could carry out precision attacks.[155]

The bombsight was developed in the 1920s and early 1930s by Carl Norden, a Dutch engineer educated in Switzerland who immigrated to the United States in 1904. The bombsight constantly calculated the bomb's trajectory based on current wind and flight conditions, which let it react quickly to changes in the wind and aircraft motion. It depended on the bombardier first sighting the target. The Mark 15 version of the sight weighed fifty pounds. Over $1.5 billion was spent on the sight's development. Ninety thousand bombsights were bought during the war. Proponents of the bombsight claimed that it could allow one to drop a bomb into a pickle barrel, and it was so highly regarded that the United States refused to allow the British to use it in early years of the war in fear that a downed plane would put the sight into the hands of the Germans.

Claims of accurate pickle-barrel bombing seldom matched reality, however. Pilots weaving to avoid flak upset the sensitive gyroscopes of the bombsight. In combat, bombadiers could not easily and calmly enter all the data necessary, and often it was not possible to see the target in the first place through all the smoke, cloud, and haze. The Eighth Air Force could never find a way to bomb with maximum precision and maximum protection.[156]

Effects and Consequences of Allied Bombing, 1942–1943—Unsustainable?

During 1942, damage to German society and economy remained limited. Weapons output expanded by over 50 percent during the year. Postwar calculations by the US Bombing Survey suggested a loss of potential overall output of 2.5 percent due to British bombing. On the other hand, the bombing did compel the German enemy to divert aircraft, guns, and ammunition to defense, when they could have been used for the fighting on the Eastern Front.[157] Another indirect effect of the bombing came from the Allied bombing of U-boat pens in France and Belgium. While this bombing did little damage, the vast diversion of concrete to protect the pens greatly slowed the building of the Atlantic Wall, the German fortifications constructed from 1942 to 1944 to confront any Allied invasion of Europe.[158] The Atlantic Wall is discussed in more detail in chapter 6 on D-Day.

During 1943, Bomber Command had some sporadic direct successes—most notably on its raid on Hamburg on July 24–25, 1943. In this raid, Bomber Command used "window" (chaff) for first time. The use of chaff involved dropping a large number of narrow strips of aluminum 30 cm long and 1.5 cm wide. This effectively blinded German radar, though, later in the year, the Germans found ways to counter the chaff. The attack caused a firestorm in the city, killing by some estimates over forty thousand people. Even so, by November 1943, the city was back to 80 percent of pre-raid output. Aside from the terrible toll of casualties, the Hamburg raid may have also given Bomber Command a false sense of what it could accomplish in city bombing, especially against targets deeper into Germany.[159]

In January 1943, both Bomber Command and the American Eighth Air Force carried out the first of a series of raids on Berlin. To counter the growing Allied bomber offensive, the Germans withdrew fighter groups from the Eastern Front for home defense. By mid-1943, the Germans had around four hundred night fighters, equipped with radar, available and five hundred day fighters. This accounted for almost 50 percent of all German fighter strength. The Germans also greatly expanded their deployment of antiaircraft guns, again diverting the weapons from fighting fronts. However, antiaircraft accounted for a considerably smaller proportion of Allied bomber losses than Luftwaffe night fighters.[160]

As a result of these German efforts, by the spring of 1943, Allied air losses rose to terrifying levels. Less than one RAF aircrew in five survived a thirty-mission tour.[161] For the United States, most crews on a tour of twenty-five or thirty operations died before they reached their total. Concern with losses reached a pitch for the Eighth Air Force in the October 14, 1943, raid on the ball-bearing factory in Schweinfurt. Sixty-five bombers were lost out of an attacking force of 229. Fighters accompanied the bombers only as far as Aachen, and this only thanks to the addition of extra fuel tanks, which pushed their range to 350 miles. So severe was the risk on any raid past fighter cover that, for the next four months, operations were carried out with increasing numbers of bombers only on cities within easy range.[162, 163] The next raid deep into Germany was made only on February 20, 1944, in very different circumstances.

Bomber Command also began to experience higher losses and, despite Oboe and H2S, continued to hit urban areas with only intermittent success. Over the course of 1943, the command lost over four thousand aircraft, 2,800 in combat.[164] Raids deep into Germany threatened to become unsustainable.

Allied Bombing 1944–1945: Turn of the Tide

As the bombing campaigns progressed in 1943, the Allies were desperate to find ways to reduce the bombing losses. That they found such ways was a tribute to science and technology. In particular, the turnaround in strategic bombing was due to three interrelated factors:

1. Measures to make it difficult for German night fighters to locate the bombers;
2. The tactical decision by the US Air Force to attack German fighter assembly plans, fighter air bases, and oil refineries; and above all,
3. The development of interceptors, with ranges long enough to accompany the bombers deep into Germany.

Measures to Blind and Spoof German Night Fighters

By 1944, the Allies realized that the radars on the bombers, H2S and the so-called Monica radar used to look for German night fighters, were instead allowing the night fighters to locate the bombers. Earlier the Allied had understood also that the IFF (Identification Friend or Foe) on the bombers could also be so used by the German fighters. Acting on this intelligence, the Allies then shut down the IFF and made minimal use of radar, thus effectively blinding the night fighters. Also the Allies used spoofing raids where a few Mosquitoes would drop chaff to mimic a large bomber force, drawing the night fighters, with diminishing fuel supplies, to the wrong area. Also after June 1944, the Allies were able to operate close to the German border, so that jamming aircraft could now operate much further forward and undertake jamming attacks against the German long-range radars. By late 1944, the German night fighter force was a wasted asset.[165]

Attacks on German Fighter Assembly Plants and Oil Production

Unlike Bomber Command, in late 1943, the United States sought a directive that made strategic sense—that bombing should contribute to making the planned invasion of Europe in 1944 possible. Its chief goal in late 1943 and early 1944 was to devastate the German fighter force so that it could not play a decisive role in the forthcoming invasion. "'Our first objective' wrote General Doolittle to his commanders on assuming control of the Eighth Air Force in January 1944, 'is to neutralize the German fighter opposition at the earliest moment.'" This was to be done by combining assaults on oil and aircraft production with calculated attrition of the German air force through air-to-air combat and fighter sweeps over German soil.[166]

Eighth and Fifteenth Air Forces in fall of 1944 had more than five thousand heavy bombers in the European theater and could call on over five thousand fighters, including by November around two thousand P-51 Mustangs (see below). Bomber Command had about 1,500 bombers (mostly Lancasters) available.[167]

United States attacks on oil and air power became decisive—more so than British area bombing. In January 1944, total German oil production and imports was 852,000 tons. In December 1944, it was 294,000 tons.[168] By spring 1944, the United States was organizing attacks on German oil and also imposing intolerable levels of attrition on the German fighter force, always seeking opportunities for combat. The combat, as discussed below, was largely done by the Mustang and to an extent by the P-47 Thunderbolt with extra fuel tanks.

The Mustang Long-Range Interceptor

In attacks deep into Germany, what was needed were single-engine fighters faster and more maneuverable than anything the Luftwaffe possessed—and with fuel range to permit flying with the bombers to Berlin and back. This seemed impossible—but it happened.[169] It happened with the marriage of the American P-51 with the British Rolls-Royce Merlin engine. The result was the Mustang, P-51, with a range of 1650 miles and a top speed of 440 mph.

In 1940, the British had put in an order for a new fighter with a young American company, North American Aviation. Employing a radical new design by its chief designer, Edgar Schmued, the company produced the P-51, which was highly maneuverable and with amazingly low drag. The plane was then tested in Britain, most decisively on April 30, 1942, by Ronnie Harker, Rolls-Royce's chief test pilot. Harker's report that if the Mustang had "... a powerful and good engine like the Merlin 61, its performance should be outstanding as it is 35 mph faster than a Spitfire V at roughly the same power" changed the course of the bombing war! Harker's assessment was validated by the Rolls-Royce mathematician Witold Challiers, and the match of the P-51 and Merlin engine was done.[170, 171]

The Mustang with a full rear tank held 269 gallons and consumed on average an astoundingly low sixty-four gallons per hour. By comparison, the Spitfire held only ninety-nine gallons; and the P-47 consumed 140 gallons per hour.[172] The reason for the Mustang's low drag was not well understood at the time, but later it was attributed to a slight concave curvature of the fuselage.

Despite the great attractions of the Mustang, some authorities in the United States opposed its deployment on a large scale. The "all powerful War Material Board in Washington, under the dogmatic Major-General Oliver P. Echols, was adamant; this was not an all-American plane, it wasn't put together here, it didn't go through the Wright Field process, and, besides, there were a further 7,500 Allison engines [made in the United States] on order and that company and its Congressman would get very mad at any cancellation."[173]

Fortunately, several influential voices came to the rescue of the Mustang. These included Assistant Secretary of War for Air Robert Lovett and Assistant Air Force Attaché Thomas Hitchcock in Great Britain. As a naval ensign during World War I, Lovett flew for a time with the British Naval Air Service on patrol and combat missions. Hitchcock was one of the world's most famous polo players, with relations in the White House and a charismatic personality. He also was a flyer, having served in the Lafayette Flying Corps in France in World War I. They and others finally convinced General Hap Arnold, chief of the US Air Force, to support a crash program, and soon the Mustang was in high production. The Merlin engines were made both in England and in America by Packard. The official US history of bombing says: "the story of the [opposition to the] P-51 came close to representing the costliest mistake made by the Army Air Force in WWII."

In addition to its great range, the Mustang was far superior to all German piston-engine fighters. It was "30–70 miles per hour faster than any German piston-engine fighter and had better acceleration, while its maneuverability, dive speed and climb rate matched or exceeded anything the Luftwaffe could offer."[174]

The role of the Mustang in the turnaround in the air war deservedly gets most attention. But the P-47 Thunderbolt and the Lockheed Lightning also played significant roles. With the Mustang able to escort the bombers all the way to Berlin and beyond, the German fighters could not simply wait, as they had before to attack the bombers after the escorts had left. And once the German fighters began to attack all along the route, it gave the short-ranged Thunderbolts especially more of an opportunity to engage.

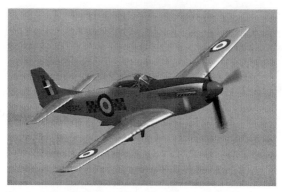

Fig. 5.2 The P-51 Mustang Interceptor. The airplane was a result of the merger of an American airframe design and the Rolls-Royce Merlin aeroengine.

Victory in the Air War

With all these developments, the change in the air war was decisive, though it wasn't so immediately. Between November 1943 and March 1944, Bomber Command lost 1,128 aircraft. And in April 1944 alone, the Eighth Air Force lost 422 heavy bombers, 25 percent of the total force.

However, the tide was already turning. The Luftwaffe was gradually—and then not so gradually—disintegrating. Between January and June 1944, German aircraft losses on all fronts included over six thousand lost in combat, and another 3,600 lost in accidents, predominantly due to poor weather or pilot error. Despite fighting much of the time over German territory, the German air force also lost over 2,200 pilots. Flying schools were under intense pressure to supply crew, and this along with persistent shortages of fuel due to Allied attacks on oil refineries meant that training time had to be drastically reduced, further undermining the ability of the German fighters to take on the Mustangs and Thunderbolts.

During that April 1944, when Allied losses were so high, the German fighter force itself lost almost half of its strength. The high losses made it difficult for Germany to keep more than five hundred serviceable fighters in the air fleet at any one time. "Missions for German pilots became all but suicidal by the time of the Normandy invasion."[175]

Despite Allied attacks, between January and June 1944, German production of fighters was almost ten thousand, not much less than Allied production. Yet the Eighth Fighter Command had more than twice the number of fighters available when compared to the Reich Air Fleet. In May 1944, the German Air Fleet had 437 serviceable fighters, the Eighth Air Force 1,174. Allied serviceability rate was higher. Also, it is striking that more than nine thousand German aircraft in 1944 were lost in transit to Allied air attack before they reached the combat squadrons.[176]

Perhaps most striking was the loss of the German fighter aces between March and June 1944, shown most graphically in an amazing table from the German history of the Luftwaffe during the war, and reproduced by Paul Kennedy. During that period, twenty-eight German aces, responsible for more than two thousand kills between them, lost their lives.[177]

With the erosion of the German fighter forces, success became evident in May and June 1944 when Allied bomber losses suddenly fell sharply from the peak in April. By the summer, the percentage of attacking bombers actually hit by enemy fighters fell from 3.7 percent in March and April to only 0.4 percent in July and August. Overall loss rates of bombers fluctuated between 1 and 2 percent throughout the period from September 1944 to the end of the war. Allied fighter losses were never high. Losses amounted to just over 1 percent of all sorties in the last eight months of the war.[178]

The Allied bombing offensive remained strong in late 1944 and 1945 as German resistance crumbled. Postwar interpretations of the last three months of the war came to regard the final flourish of bombing as merely punitive, neither necessary nor, as a result, morally justified.[179] Thus for example, the Bomber Command attack on Dresden of February 13–14, 1945, caused a firestorm that killed

25,000 civilians for no apparent purpose. But this line of argument is perhaps a little in hindsight. One reason for the continued pressure on the Germans was fear that new German weapons could reverse the military situation. Another fear was the unleashing of chemical or biological weapons. At the time, there was still a perceived menace from the Germans.

Effects of the Bombing

The US Strategic Bombing Survey (USSBS) concluded that city area attack did little to reduce German output but that attacks on oil and communication links in the last two years of the war markedly restricted flying time for German aircraft both in combat and in training, contributing significantly to the destruction of the German air force in 1944 and 1945. The postwar British survey concluded similarly. Germans interviewed after the war pretty much agreed with these conclusions.

Area bombing was nevertheless, despite its critics, not entirely without impact on the German war effort.[180] The bombing did have the impact of distorting German strategy. "In early 1943, nearly 60 percent of German fighters were in the Western theater facing the bombing; in January, nearly 70 percent; by October 1944, 80 percent. ... in the summer of 1944 there were 2172 batteries of light and heavy anti-aircraft artillery on the home front, but only 443 batteries in the Mediterranean theater, and 300 on the whole of the Eastern Front. The anti-aircraft service absorbed 250,000 people in 1940 and almost a million at its peak in 1944."[181]

So the indirect effects of the bombing were substantial. But it is also true that the Allied bombing strategy imposed opportunity costs on the Allies. Instead of the massive buildup of bombers, the Allies could have devoted more resources to building landing craft for the invasion of France—a lack of such craft delayed the invasion. Most compellingly, far more aircraft could have been assigned to the Battle of the Atlantic than was done, and far sooner. This has been put most strongly by Williamson Murray:

> What is even more astonishing, half a century after the war, was the obdurate unwillingness of the Allied air forces to devote the resources necessary to close the gap in the air cover over the Central Atlantic. Except for Coastal Command, the RAF leadership opposed the commitment of long-range aircraft to protecting convoys with a fervor that bordered on fanaticism ... [until] their political masters forced their hand.[182]

Moral Dilemmas

Allied strategic bombing has always raised questions of morality. When can the deliberate killing of civilians be justified? We cannot in this chapter truly explore this deep question, but a few points that have framed the debate may be mentioned.

One such point is the difference between the British explicit decision to bomb cities, in part to destroy civilian morale, and the American decision to aim at specific industrial targets, although it was understood that in doing so, many civilians would be killed and injured. The Americans have always maintained the moral high ground here—that it was right not to target civilians deliberately. Others call this moral hairsplitting.[183]

A second point, made for example by the political philosopher and author of *Just and Unjust Wars*, Michael Walzer, argues that even indiscriminate bombing of cities could be justified at a time when such bombing was the only way to confront the evil of the Nazis, but no longer justified when the possibility of Nazi victory disappeared.

It does seem to me that the more certain a German victory appeared to be in the absence of a bomber offensive, the more justifiable was the decision to launch the offensive. … Suppose that civilization itself is really at stake, that the question is not the price of victory, but simply victory simply, and our defeat will be a triumph not for some conventional them, but specifically for the Nazis. … It is not morally possible to accept the risks [of indiscriminate bombing] as soon as the threat of immeasurable evil passes. … That is why it is so easy to condemn the attack on Dresden in 1945, which killed so many thousands of people and may or may not have hastened the end of the war by a few days: there was no longer even a remote chance of a Nazi victory.[184]

Contrary views have been expressed by General Curtis LeMay, who led bombing missions in Europe and then later in Japan, and others engaged in strategic bombing. To them a warrior cannot worry about morality. A soldier has to fight and cannot concern himself overly with enemy deaths.

German Rockets and Jets

Germany also attacked the enemy's homeland in bombing raids during and after the Battle of Britain in 1940 and early 1941. It did not do so on a significant scale then again until 1944, when it again attacked Britain, this time including with the V-1 pilotless aircraft and the V-2 long-range rocket, the so-called Vergeltungswaffen or revenge weapons designed for terror bombing of London. Near the end of the war, the Germans also deployed an advanced jet fighter, the Me-262.

V-1 Pilotless Aircraft

The V-1 was developed at Peenemunde, an island in the North Sea, during the early 1940s. It was a pilotless aircraft powered by a pulsejet internal combustion engine, carrying about 150 gallons of gasoline. It was capable of being launched by ground ejectors or from aircraft. It contained a crude guidance system capable of directing the aircraft to London but not to more specific targets. Its range was limited and able to reach London only from coastal batteries along the French and Dutch coasts; also it flew at a constant speed at a relatively low altitude of about five thousand feet, making it highly vulnerable to antiaircraft fire.

It was first fired on London in the middle of June 1944, a week after D-Day, from launch sites along the French and Dutch coasts. At its peak, more than one hundred V-1s a day were fired at southeast England, about ten thousand in total, decreasing in number as sites were overrun until October 1944, when the last V-1 site in range of Britain was overrun by the Allies. After this, the V-1s were directed at the port of Antwerp and other targets in Belgium, with 2,500 V-1s being launched.

The launches against London were met by a variety of countermeasures, including barrage balloons, fighter aircraft, and, above all, antiaircraft guided by radar and employing proximity fuses. These measures were so successful that by August 1944, about four-fifths of V-1s were being destroyed.

The proximity fuse, developed in Britain and the United States, was revolutionary. Up to its use, an explosive shell aimed at incoming aircraft would detonate only upon contact with its target or at some preset altitude. But both had drawbacks. Direct hit was difficult against fast flying targets, and it was generally not clear at what altitude explosions should be timed.

The proximity fuse worked by radar. The projectile with fuse transmits a radio wave, with the amplitude of the reflected signal and the rapidity in change of amplitude indicating the closeness of the target.[185] This effect then allows the fuse to detonate an explosive device automatically when the distance to the target becomes smaller than some predetermined value or when the fuse and target pass each other. Naturally, the fuse had to be extremely rugged, able to work despite being shot out of guns at high velocity. During the war, the American electronics industry produced over twenty million fuses.

When combined with ground radars that could efficiently track the low and steady flying V-1s, the proximity fuse had stunning impact, contributing to neutralizing the V-1 attacks. The fuse is also credited with helping to counter the Japanese kamikaze attacks in the Pacific, and to effective use against German armor in the Battle of the Bulge in December 1944.

The V-2 Rocket

From early in the war, the Germans, under the leadership of Werner von Braun, sought to develop rockets that could strike long-distance targets. By 1944, von Braun had achieved success in the development of the A-4 rocket, soon to be named the V-2, revenge weapon. It had a range of over two hundred miles with an explosive warhead of one ton.

The rocket was first developed at Peenemunde. But after the RAF bombed the site in August 1943, the Germans shifted production of the rocket to Nordhausen in the Harz Mountains. Production was done deep underground in appalling conditions by workers who were prisoners of war in concentration camps, leading to many deaths by starvation and illness. More persons were killed making the V-2 than it turned out were killed by the V-2 in attacks on cities.

The rocket was forty-six feet in length and weighed about 12.5 metric tons when fully loaded. At its heart was a chamber that burnt a mixture of liquid oxygen and alcohol at a rate of about one ton every seven seconds, driving a turbine. The exhaust gases coming out of the turbine at high speed propel the rocket forward, in the same manner that when air is let out of a balloon, the balloon goes in the opposite direction of the air.

It is conservation of momentum that is at play. The momentum (velocity times mass) of the exhaust gases leaving the rocket at high velocity from the back drives the rocket mass forward at increasing velocity. Another way to say this is that the rate of change of the exhaust gases shot out of the back of the rocket times the velocity of the gases must equal the mass of the rocket times the rate of change of the rocket velocity. "Velocity" is a vector—that is, it has direction as well as magnitude. Thus if the velocity of the exhaust gases is directed out the back of the rocket, conservation of momentum demands that the change in velocity of the rocket—its acceleration—must be forward.

$$\Delta m \times v = M \times \Delta V$$

The rocket included a guidance system near the front of the rocket, and a warhead in the nose cone. Although the guidance system utilizing gyroscopes was an impressive achievement for the time, the rocket was still quite inaccurate, with an estimated Circular Probable Error (CEP) of seven miles. That is, about one half of the V-2s would fall within a circle of radius seven miles, and half outside that circle.

From June 1944 until early 1945, when the western most V-2 launching sites in the Netherlands and on the Rhine were overrun by the Allies, the V-2 rained down over London, killing over 2,700 Londoners and injuring another ten thousand.[186]

The entire V-2 program was a tremendous waste of resources for the Germans. "The U.S. strategic bombing survey estimated that the industrial effort and resources devoted to these revenge weapons equaled production of 24,000 fighter aircraft. ... Measured against its return on investment, the V-2 was undoubtedly the most cost ineffective weapon of the war."[187] Nevertheless, von Braun in the postwar era became a leading designer of rockets for the United States.

Jet Aircraft

The principle of the aircraft turbojet is for a quantity of air to be drawn in, mixed with a fuel in a combustion chamber, expanded through a turbine to drive the air compressor, and expelled through jet nozzles out of the back of the aircraft, providing a forward thrust. Development of the jet took place in Great Britain, most prominently by Frank Whittle, a young RAF officer, and in Germany by Han von Ohain.

Based on the early work of Whittle and Ohain, development of jet aircraft went forward in both countries, with the Germans slightly ahead. The Germans gave a contract for a twin-engine aircraft fitted with axial jets to Willy Messerschmitt, and this became the fighter, the Me-262. A prototype was flown in May 1943. But possibly partly because Hitler at first ordered the plane to be produced mainly as a bomber, although 564 jets were produced in 1944, the first Me-262 squadron didn't go into service until November 1944.[188]

By then it was too late to have decisive impact on the war. The plane experienced various engineering difficulties. It was difficult to fly, a serious problem given the shortage of trained pilots, and its availability was severely limited by a growing lack of aviation fuel in 1945 due to Allied attacks on fuel production.

The Gloster Meteor turbojet based on Whittle's designs became available in 1944 and had some limited success on a small scale against the German V-1s. There is no record of any combat between Meteors and Me-262s.[189]

Summary

In summary, the American and British strategic bombing of Germany (and of satellite and occupied countries) up to 1944 had limited direct effects on German war production but did have significant indirect impacts, largely by diverting substantial resources and armaments from the Mediterranean and Eastern Fronts. In 1944 and 1945, the bombing became more sharply directed at oil and aircraft production in Germany and increasingly effective. The human costs of the bombing campaigns were terrible. It has been estimated that the combined Allied bombing offensives killed an estimated six hundred thousand Germans, largely civilian, and over sixty thousand French citizens and fifty thousand Italians. Over seven million Germans were made homeless. (The German bombing of London and other British cities killed over forty thousand.)

The costs were terrible also for the Allies. In the bombing campaigns, the US and British air forces each lost as many as eighty thousand men. Given such losses, by November 1943, both US and RAF losses in raids deep into Germany looked unsustainable, mainly due to a lack of fighter escorts accompanying the bombers. However, starting in late 1943, there was a dramatic turnaround, due in large part to the introduction of the P-51 Mustang, a fighter with the range to accompany the bombers to Berlin and back.

With the advent of the Mustang, attacks deep into Germany and East Europe in 1944 and 1945 became more telling, largely destroying the Luftwaffe, with many of its most decorated pilots killed, in its vain attempts to confront the bombers, and also severely impacting German oil production critical to the German war effort. The reversal of fortune in the skies over Germany came just in time to ensure complete Allied air superiority for the forthcoming assault on France.

While the Mustang and an array of radio guidance systems were critical technical achievements of the Allies, the Germans also innovated—most dramatically in the development of the V-1 pilotless aircraft, the V-2 rocket, and the Me-262 jet aircraft. But the Allies invented ways to blunt the impact of the V-1, in part due to the invention and deployment of the proximity fuse. And the V-2, while an impressive technological achievement, was a tremendous waste of resources. The Me-262 jet came too late in the war to have much effect, and what effect it did have was limited by a severe lack of aviation fuel.

While the Allied strategic bombing raises troubling moral questions, which we noted above, the Combined Bomber Offensive played a significant role in the defeat of Nazi Germany. One additional point could be made in support of the strategic bombing. As terrible as it was on the home fronts of Germany and later Japan, it could perhaps be credited with contributing to the destruction of the deep militarization of the German and (later) Japanese societies that led to the war. This may have been the most important consequence of all of the bombing.

Bibliography

Beevor, Antony. *The Second World War,* chapter 29, "The Battle of the Atlantic and Strategic Bombing." Back Bay Books, 1987.

Birch, David. *Rolls-Royce and the Mustang,* Historical Series No. 9. Rolls-Royce Historical Trust, 1987.

Evans, Richard. *The Third Reich: Germany at War,* chapter 8, "The Last Spark of Hope." Penguin, 2008.

Jones, R.V. *Most Secret War.* Hamish Hamilton, 1978.

Hartcup, Guy. *The Effect of Science on the Second World War,* chapter 3, "Diverse Applications of Radio and Radar," and chapter 9, "Premature Weapons—The Rocket and the Jet." Palgrave, 2003.

Kennedy, Paul. *Engineers of Victory,* chapter 4, "How to Win Command of the Air." Random House, 2003.

Ludwig, Paul. *Development of the P-51 Long-Range Escort Fighter Mustang.* Classic, 2003.

Murray, Williamson, and Alan Millett. *A War to Be Won: Fighting the Second World War,* chapter 12, "The Combined Bomber Offensive." Belknap, 2000.

Overy, Richard. *The Bombers and the Bombed,* chapters 1, 2, and 3. Penguin, 2013.

Overy, Richard. *Why the Allies Won,* chapter 4, "The Means to Victory, Bombers and Bombing." Pimlico, 2006.

Film

The Memphis Belle—directed by William Wyler (1944), the story of a B-17 and its crew in bombing raids over Germany.

CHAPTER 6

D-Day

Planning

During the last months of 1943 and early months of 1944, the American and British combined command planned for the invasion of the continent. For the invasion, General Dwight Eisenhower was appointed supreme commander, with subordinate American and British commanders in charge of naval, air, and ground operations. The challenge was daunting. Under the energetic direction of General Erwin Rommel, commander of the army group tasked with strengthening the Atlantic Wall, the Germans had undertaken a massive construction program that sowed millions of mines, built thousands of coastal and field fortifications, and installed huge numbers of anti-boat obstacles along the beaches.[190] What had to be launched was the greatest amphibious operation in history against the most strongly defended coastline that any force had ever tried to assault.[191]

Fig. 6.1 One Element of the Atlantic Wall—The Gun Placements, Mines, and Obstacles the Germans Emplaced along the Coastline of France

Strategic Choices

The strategic choices facing both the Allies and the Germans were grave. For the Allies, the first critical decision was where on the coast of Western Europe to aim the invasion. The Pas de Calais in France across from the cliffs of Dover at the narrowest part of the English Channel was one possibility. In addition to the shorter distance from England, it had the attraction of being closest to Germany once a lodgment could be secured. However, at the end, the Allies decided on Normandy. At the Pas de Calais, the Germans would be able to counterattack from three directions, while at Normandy they could only do so from the south. In addition, Normandy had wider beaches and also offered the Allies the prospect of eventual use of the port of Cherbourg.[192]

For the Germans, the strategic conundrum was whether to concentrate its mobile tank divisions close to the possible landing areas with the intent of beating back the invasion in the early hours, or to station these divisions farther away from the beaches in reserve, ready to move rapidly after the landings had commenced. Rommel advocated the first strategy, while the person in overall charge of the Western Front, Field Marshal Gerd von Rundstadt, supported the second. The result was a compromise. Three armored divisions were assigned to each army group. Four armored groups were held back as a mobile reserve to be sent to the critical point once the location of the main assault was known—but these units were allowed to move only with permission of Hitler's headquarters.[193]

For the Allies, it was essential that they achieve control of the seas and the air before the invasion to allow shipments of men and resources from the United States to England, and to guard the invasion fleet in the English Channel during the assault on Europe. As chronicled in the preceding chapters, this was accomplished with marked success in the months preceding the invasion.

Beyond that, it was critical to somehow overcome the great superiority in the number of German divisions in Western Europe compared to the number of divisions the Allies could deploy in the first hours and days of the invasion. Germany had fifty-eight divisions in France and the Low Countries, some of them static, but many tank divisions highly mobile that could be directed to the beaches once the Germans knew where the landings were taking place. The initial assault by the Allies would consist of five army and three airborne divisions aimed at securing a lodgment area on five beaches in Normandy—so it was critical that the exact time and place of the invasion be kept secret, that the beach fortifications at the landing sites somehow be dismantled and neutralized, that the ability of the Germans to bring forces to the beachhead be severely degraded, and that means be found to bring supplies to the beachheads rapidly despite there being no natural port that could be used. In all these respects, the Allies succeeded, a story told below. As in other aspects of the war, science and technology played prominent roles.

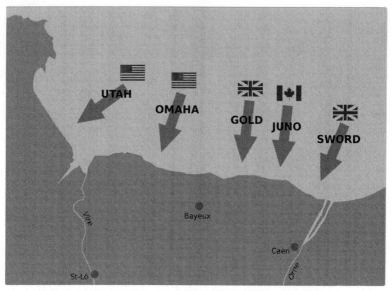

Fig. 6.2. The D-Day Beaches. Each beach was five to eight kilometers, and the total distance from the western-most beach to the eastern was about one hundred kilometers. (T. Daniel Feiveson)

Deception

To keep the Germans unsure of the time and place of the main Allied assault, the Allies mounted a brilliant deception campaign to persuade the German High Command that some landing would take place in Norway, and that the main assault would be at the Pas de Calais, across the narrowest part of the English Channel, and that any landing at Normandy would be merely a diversionary feint. Ultra was critical in reassuring Allied intelligence that the ruse was working.

The key deception campaigns were termed Fortitude North and Fortitude South. Fortitude North was the code name for the plan to convince the Germans that there might be an invasion of Norway at the time of D-Day. It was aimed to take advantage of Hitler's obsession with Scandinavia, whose control by the Germans he believed critical. As a result, the Germans kept strong forces stationed in Norway.

To persuade the Germans to keep these forces there, the Allies created a fictitious British Fourth Army of over three hundred thousand men stationed in Scotland preparing for an invasion. This was done by a variety of means. For one, the intelligence organizations simulated the sort of wireless traffic the Germans would expect from a large army. By spring 1944, the air over Scotland was alive with messages in cipher and in plaintext. Calculated leaks to the press also amplified the deception. For example, local newspapers wrote of Fourth Army football matches, a major in Fourth Army was to be married, and so on. In addition, the RAF increased photoreconnaissance flights over Norway, and Russian fictional submarines were reported in the vicinity of the invasion coast. Also neutral Sweden became a target in the deception campaign, with diplomatic threats to Sweden warning of what the Allies would do if they occupied Sweden.

Fortitude North was a great success. Hitler not only kept forces in Norway, he reinforced them. By late spring of 1944, Germany had thirteen divisions stationed in Norway, over four hundred thousand men, including ninety thousand naval and sixty thousand air personnel, one panzer division, and an air force. These forces were kept in Norway until the end of the war.[194]

Fortitude South was the code name for the operation to convince the Germans that the main D-Day invasion would occur at the Pas de Calais. This was done through the establishment of a fictitious army group opposite the Pas de Calais, a pattern of bombing that focused more on Pas de Calais than on Normandy, and the imaginative use of double agents.

The phantom army (First US Army Group—FUSAG) would consist of one Canadian and three American divisions, and one Canadian armored division. Four armored and four infantry American divisions would constitute a follow-up force. And behind them, fifty divisions in the United States were reported to be awaiting shipment to the Pas de Calais after FUSAG established a beachhead.[195]

To simulate this army, the Allies created wireless transmissions similar to what might be expected from a gathering army and fabricated tank parks, petrol dumps, hospitals, pipelines, and sewage farms much as Hollywood might create a film set, out of lumber, rubber, wire, and cardboard.[196] Thousands of inflatable full-sized tanks and trucks were openly arrayed while an effective total blackout was imposed across the counties where the real invasion armies lay.[197] Lieutenant General George Patton, the American commander the Germans feared the most, was designated commander of FUSAG and took his station in the part of England closest to the Pas de Calais in a way the Germans would be sure to discover.

Above all, the Allies utilized a remarkable group of double agents to confirm to the Germans the existence of FUSAG and Pas de Calais as the focus of an invasion. At the time of D-Day, the Allies controlled twenty such agents in Britain, all of them feeding information to their German handlers. In the weeks leading up to the invasion, the Allies relied mainly on four of the twenty double agents, code-named Garbo, Brutus, Tricycle, and Treasure. Garbo, a Spaniard who had earlier worked in Lisbon feeding the Germans bogus information, convinced the Germans that he had some dozen other operative working for him across the country. Brutus had been an officer in the Polish General Staff. Tricycle was a Yugoslav, and Treasure was a Frenchwoman.[198]

The final elements of the deception were a bombing campaign in France that dropped more bombs in the Pas de Calais region than in the Normandy region and a spoofing operation on D-Day to simulate a large movement of ships toward the Pas de Calais, which we elaborate below.

Fortitude South also was a stunning success. By June, the

German Seventh Army in Normandy had fourteen divisions—one division every 120 miles of coast. By contrast, near Pas de Calais, there were twenty divisions—one division every fifty miles.[199] Still more remarkably, Fortitude South kept the Germans off balance even after the Normandy invasion. It convinced the Germans that another landing was to take place at the Pas de Calais and tied up large numbers of German troops and armor long after D-Day. It is striking that Colonel Alexis von Roenne, chief of German intelligence, late on D-Day sent out a message that "the landing operation in Normandy will certainly not be the only attempted major landing by the Allies. A second such attack must be expected definitely in the Pas de Calais and therefore a withdrawal of troops from that sector cannot be allowed."[200] Von Roenne was later executed by Hitler as being complicit in the plot to assassinate him.

Unfortunately, in the secret and complex war of double agents, there was a still unexplained error of potentially grave consequences by the Allies that gave away a planned message to the French underground resistance on the eve of the D-Day invasion. The Germans had discovered that on the first and fifteenth of the month of a planned invasion, the first line of a couplet by the French poet, Verlaine, was to be sent out; the second line would then be transmitted within forty-eight hours of the actual invasion.[201]

The couplet was: The long sobs of the violins of autumn/ Soothes my heart with a monotonous languor.*

The first line was transmitted by radio at beginning of May—and of course nothing happened, and this did make the Germans somewhat unsure how serious the Verlaine messages were. But the first line was transmitted again in June, and then the second line on the actual eve of invasion. This put one German army on

---

* Les sanglots longs des violins d'automne/Bercent mon Coeur d'une langueur monotone.

high alert but was mostly ignored by the German Seventh Army in Normandy, a welcome break for the Allies.

One other curious episode in the intelligence war should be mentioned. In *Daily Telegraph* crossword puzzles in the month prior to the invasion, several words associated with the invasion were mentioned, including the names of all the beaches, the code name for D-Day, "overlord," and "mulberry." This was noticed, and the crossword compilers were questioned by MI-5, British counterintelligence, who determined that the appearance of the words was innocent. But apparently it was not just a random coincidence. Over sixty years later, a former student of one of the compilers reported that this compiler frequently requested words from his students, many of whom were children in the same area as US military personnel and most probably had heard mention of the words.

Breaching the Atlantic Wall

For the invasion itself, the combined staff determined that it be done at dawn and at low tide but with rising tides such that the following forces could be brought in on a second tide before nightfall. See the box on tides. The reason for the assault at low tide was so that minesweepers and demolition units could demolish underwater obstacles that the Germans had emplaced along the coast of France. The Allies also determined that the invasion should begin on a night with a late-rising moon that would keep the initial moves of the invasion force shrouded in darkness at the start but then allow some visibility for the drop of airborne units behind enemy lines in the early morning of D-Day. On June 6, the moon rose between 1 and 2 a.m. The necessity of meeting all these goals—tides and moonlight—limited the days of the month to a very few. The date chosen was June 5 but, as noted below, delayed a day until June 6 due to inclemet weather.[202]

Tides

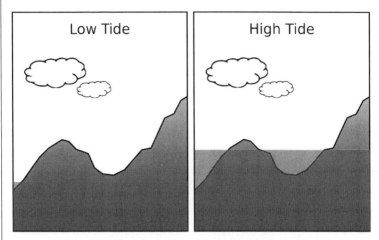

*Fig. 6.3 The Tidal Range, Which Determined the
Timing of the Invasion (T. Daniel Feiveson)*

Tides are the periodic rise and fall of waters in the ocean, produced by the attraction of primarily the moon but also the sun, occurring about every twelve hours. The vertical distance between high tide and low tide is called the tidal range. The greatest tidal ranges are when the sun, earth, and moon are in line—a new or full moon. These are called spring tides. The tidal range is less when the sun, earth, and moon are perpendicular to one another—called neap tides. See figure. In some places, such as Nova Scotia, the tidal range can be fifty feet or higher because of the conformation of the coast. On the D-Day beaches, the tidal range was about six meters or twenty feet.

A six-meter range meant that the water would rise at about one meter per hour. The times of low water and the rate of rise had to be known precisely to give the demolition units the time to do their work in blowing up the beach obstacles. This calculation is complicated because ocean tides vary in timing and height, not only due to the sun-moon alignment but also how they intersect the shoreline. In fact, the low-water times were different at the five landing beaches. Between the westernmost beach, Utah, and the most eastern, Sword, separated by about 100 km, the difference in low-water time was about one hour. So the landing time at each beach would have to be staggered according to the tide predictions.

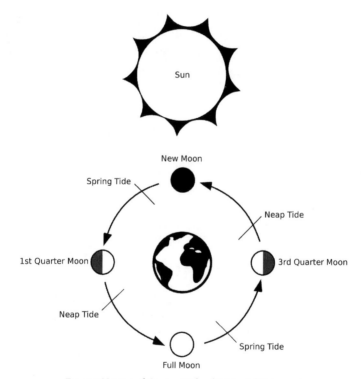

Fig. 6.4 Neap and Spring Tides (T. Daniel Feiveson)

Spring tides are when the sun and the moon are in a line, as shown in figure 6.4. Neap tides are when they are at right angles to each other.

Command of the sea and air enabled Allied planners to follow Rommel's intensive preparations step by step. As described by Chester Wilmot, a war correspondent who covered and then wrote extensively of the invasion, "Reconnaissance planes mapped the German progress with aerial photographs ... naval survey parties in midget submarines and small craft charted coast line, sea-bed, and mine fields off-shore. Commandoes landed by night to examine beaches and fortifications. Inland a close watch on German dispositions and defenses was kept by agents parachuted into France and by men and women of the French resistance."[203]

To confront the barriers and mines set by Rommel, the Allies launched 255 minesweeping vessels on D-Day and also adopted various ingenious technologies. Chief among them was the development of tanks with special functions, the brainchild of Major General Percy Hobart. Some American Sherman and British Churchill tanks, for example, were fitted with flotation devices to make the tanks amphibious; others were fitted with flails where gigantic metal chains beat the sand and exploded enemy mines; some were equipped with massive wire cutters and bull-dozer blades; and still others carried their own rolled-up metal or wooden bridges that allowed the crossing of ditches and tank traps.[204] Later, in preparation for the breakout from Normandy, tanks were equipped with giant front teeth that could rip through the hedgerows of Normandy, allowing the tanks to race across open fields.

Planners had also to address a range of other problems in which scientists and engineers figured prominently. For example, they had to devise a suite of amphibious vehicles to bring troops, tanks, and armor onto the beaches. And the entire Normandy region had to be mapped in great detail. In preparation of the airborne landings, the British army constructed a detailed model of the Orne Valley, correct even to the height of the trees and the size of the houses, from which model the RAF made a film to show the pilots who would be in the vanguard of the air assault.[205]

The planners sought also to find ways to knock out or jam as many of the German coastal radars as possible. To this end, the counterintelligence unit under the direction of R.V. Jones collected a comprehensive description of every German coastal radar station, including maps and high- and low-level photographs, in sufficient detail for accurate attacks to be planned.[206] The dossier covered a very much wider coastline than just Normandy, so that if any leakage of information should occur, the Germans would have no clue regarding the selected area.

Starting in May, fighter attacks on the radars commenced, with great success. Not only were the German radars largely eliminated but so too were the jammers that the Germans could have used to confuse Allied radar. Of the forty-seven radar stations that were in operation three weeks before D-Day, hardly more than a half a dozen were able to transmit on D-Day, and these were so shaken up that their operators fell easily for a British spoof that the main invasion was to be against the Pas de Calais.

The spoof aimed at giving the impression that a large seaborne force was headed toward landings east of the Seine. This was done by flying aircraft across the channel in orbits such that the center point of each orbit moved in a southeasterly direction at a rate of eight knots, the speed of a seaborne convoy. Chaff to confuse the German radar would be dropped the whole time.[207] In addition, radar echo simulators were carried on motor launches to give augmented echoes so that a few ships traveling under the chaff cloud would, it was hoped, appear as a massive convoy to any airborne radar reconnaissance that the Germans might employ.

Weather

The one critical factor out of the hand of the planners was the weather. Minimum conditions: surface winds not exceeding Force 3 (8–12 mph) on shore nor Force 4 (13–18 mph) offshore, visibility at least three miles, half moonlight for the airborne landings. To ensure the best possible predictions, the Allies had established five hundred weather stations across the UK and eight ships in the Atlantic taking hourly weather readings.[208]

Predicted stormy conditions postponed the invasion initially set for Monday, June 5. Group Captain John Stagg, the RAF meteorologist in charge, recalled that on June 2, "In all the charts for the 40 or 50 years I had examined I could not recall one which at this time of the year remotely resembled this chart in the number and intensity of depressions it portrayed at one time."[209]

The decision to delay the invasion was made in calm weather, and then with the predicted storm raging on Sunday, June 4, Stagg projected a period of calmer weather approaching, allowing the invasion now to be set for Tuesday, June 6. (The June 6 date for D-Day is well known; not everyone realizes that June 6, 1944, was a Tuesday. For the amusement of some who may be interested, a box at the end of this chapter provides a relatively simple algorithm to find the day of the week once given the date.)

The ragged weather, it turned out, was fortunate since the Germans believed that the disturbed weather in the channel would persist throughout the current phase of the moon and tides, and they relaxed their vigilance.[210] This was confirmed in an Ultra intercept on June 4 in which the Luftwaffe predicted that the disturbed weather in the channel would persist throughout the current phase of the moon and tides.

The Invasion

Three airborne divisions were parachuted over the Normandy countryside in the early morning of June 6. Many of the drops missed their targets and were more spread out than planned. But because the drops were so dispersed, they had the effect of confusing the Germans about the location of the Allied attack.

Putting five land divisions onto the European continent in a single day required a vast armada of ships and aircraft. Over seven thousand naval vessels contributed, including 138 warships, 221 escort vessels, 287 minesweepers, and over four thousand amphibious craft. In the air, 11,590 military aircraft supported the invasion.[211] It took brilliant leadership by Admiral Bertram Ramsay, commander of Allied naval forces, to coordinate this armada, leaving from a score of ports along the British coast to arrive before Normandy at the break of dawn on D-Day.[212]

The deception plan, aided by the break in the weather, had been stunningly effective. "[N]o submarine, no aircraft, no radar set—not one officer or one man of the mighty Wehrmacht—detected the advance of the biggest force of warships in history."[213]

Starting at dawn, the Allies landed five divisions on five beaches the first day.* Despite fierce resistance, especially on Omaha Beach, 155,000 troops were landed on French soil on the first day, including 23,000 airborne forces. The costs were high. On Omaha Beach alone, approximately 2,500 Americans lost their lives. However, by the end of the day, the Allies had secured control of a lodgment area sufficient to bring in troops and supplies.

The Allies were aware that the costs would be substantial. They had in their forces in England eight thousand doctors, six hundred thousand doses of penicillin, fifty tons of sulfa drugs, and eight hundred thousand pints of plasma.[214]

---

* As noted earlier, the two most western beaches, Utah and Omaha, were American targets. In the center, Gold was British. To the east, Juno was Canadian, and Sword was British.

Fig. 6.5 Juno Beach, D-Day (Courtesy of Imperial War Museum)

The Mulberry Artificial Harbors

To allow the landing of the massive numbers of men, vehicles, and resources in the days after the invasion without a natural port, the Allies concocted an amazing alternative—the establishment of two massive artificial harbors to be floated out to the beaches, the so-called Mulberries. One was constructed opposite Omaha Beach and one opposite Gold. Their contribution was vital. Both were constructed by June 9, just three days after D-Day. By the second week, the Allies had landed half a million troops with attendant equipment, and by July had landed over one million men and nearly two hundred thousand vehicles.[215]

Fig. 6.6 A Mulberry Artificial Harbor (Courtesy of Imperial War Museum)

The Mulberries contained all the elements intrinsic to any harbor: breakwater, piers, roadways, and so on. Ships were towed across the English Channel and sunk. Each harbor required over six hundred thousand tons of concrete and had ten miles of floating roadways. Though a severe storm in the channel on June 19 destroyed the American harbor at Omaha, the British Mulberry saw heavy duty for six months after D-Day.[216]

Stopping German Reinforcement

At the same time as the Allied flow of men and machines to the shore were underway, it was critical to blunt German reinforcement moving to the beaches. The stage for this task was set in the weeks before the invasion, where a massive bombing campaign took out bridges, rail yards, and other transportation nodes. The tactics of the campaign were worked out, in part, by scientists working closely with the military. By June 5, of twenty-four road and rail bridges over the Seine, eighteen had been destroyed, three damaged, and the other three so under attack that they could not be used in daylight. After D-Day, relentless air strikes on German movements during daylight also sharply limited German mobility. By June, rail traffic had declined to 30 percent of January's total; by early July, it had declined to 10 percent.[217] In addition, members of the French resistance sabotaged countless rail yards and other transportation nodes, severely degrading German mobility.[218]

Conclusion

To a remarkable degree, all the significant challenges facing the Allies were successfully met: deception to keep the Germans uncertain of where the main invasion would be launched; measures to disable the massive German obstacles at the beaches; assembly of artificial harbors to allow shipment across the channel of men, vehicles, and resources; and the bombing of transportation nodes to slow German movement of armor to the beaches. In the end, the Normandy invasion was a great strategic victory that led to the liberation of France and set the stage for the final destruction of Nazi Germany.

Days of the Week

As noted, D-Day was June 6, 1944. This was a Tuesday. And in this box, we explain how one can find the day of the week from the date. This scheme is due to John Conway, a professor of mathematics, emeritus, at Princeton University. For simplicity, we look only at dates in the twentieth and twenty-first centuries.

Consider the last day of February as "doomsday." Once we know that day, the following dates will also be the same doomsday:

4/4, 6/6, 8/8, 10/10, 12/12, 5/9 and 9/5, 7/11 and 11/7, 3/0, 1/24 on a regular year, and 1/25 on a leap year.

The next step is to find out when doomsday is for any given year. The trick here is as follows:

For 1900, it is Wednesday.

For 2000, it is Tuesday

Then consider any other year. Divide the year past the century mark by twelve, add the remainder, and add the remainder divided by four, ignoring any remainder. Then add that number to the 1900 or 2000 doomsday.

For example, take the year 1944.

44/12 = 3 with 8 remainder. 8/4 = 2. So number is 3 + 8 + 2 = 13. Doomsday for 1944 is then Wednesday + 13 = Tuesday.

Remember that if Tuesday is doomsday, then so is 6/6. So June 6, 1944, was a Tuesday.

Let us look at another well-known date from the war, December 7, 1941.

41/12 = 3 + 5 remainder; 5/4 = 1. So sum is 3 + 5 + 1 = 9. Wednesday + 9 = Friday. So Doomsday in 1941 is Friday.

Remember then that 12/12 is a Friday, and therefore also is 12/5. Then 12/7 must be Friday + 2 = Sunday. December 7, 1941, the day of Pearl Harbor is thus a Sunday, which of course we already knew.

Take one more example. Let us say 9/11/2001.

1/12 = 0 with 1 remainder. 1 divided by 4 = 0. So doomsday for 2001 = Tuesday + 1 = Wednesday.

Remember then that 9/5 is also a Wednesday, which means that 9/12 is a Wednesday also. So 9/11 is a Tuesday.

Bibliography

Atkinson, Rick. *The Guns at Last Light*. Henry Holt and Company, 2013.

Beevor, Antony. *The Second World War*. Back Bay Books, 2012.

Brown, Anthony Cave. *Bodyguard of Lies*. Quill/William Morrow, 1975.

Hess, Gary. *The United States at War, 1941–1945*. Wiley-Blackwell, 2011.

Jones, R.V. *Most Secret War*. Hamish Hamilton, 1978.

Kennedy, Paul. *Engineers of Victory*. Random House, 2013.

McIntyre, Ben. *Double Cross: The True Story of D-Day Spies*. Crown, 2012.

Murray, Williamson, and Allan Millett. *A War to Be Won*. Belknap Press, 2000.

Olson, Lynne. *Last Hope Island*. Random House, 2017.

Overy, Richard. *Why the Allies Won*. Pimlico, 2006.

Weinberg, Gerhard. *A World at Arms*. Cambridge University Press, 2005.

Wilmot, Chester. *The Struggle for Europe*. Harper and Brothers, 1952.

Film

The Longest Day—directed by Darryl Zanuck and others (1962), the docudrama of D-Day.

CHAPTER 7

— ⚛ —

The Making of the Atomic Bomb

History of Fission

In 1904, at a talk to the Corps of Royal Engineers in London, a young physicist, Frederick Soddy, made a startling statement:

> It is probable that all heavy matter possesses—latent and bound up with the structure of the atom—a similar quantity of energy to that possessed by radium. If it could be tapped and controlled, what an agent it would be in shaping the world's destiny! The man who put his hand on the lever by which a parsimonious nature regulates so jealously the output of this store of energy would possess a weapon by which he could destroy the earth if he chose.[219]

Soddy later put these thoughts into a paper, and inspired by Soddy's words, the writer H.G. Wells wrote a novel, *A World Set Free*, which imagined a world nuclear war and then in the wake of the war, the development of civilian nuclear power leading to a great renaissance for the world.

This novel inspired a young Hungarian physicist, Leo Szilard, to ponder how nuclear energy could be released on a large scale, and in London in 1933, he conceived the idea of a chain reaction, started in a manner at that time wholly speculative.

In the years following, the physicist Enrico Fermi in Italy, the French physicists, Irene Curie (daughter of Marie) and her husband, Frederick Joliot, at the Radium Institute in Paris, and others began to unlock the mysteries of the heavy matter that Soddy alluded to by bombarding the heavy element uranium with neutrons. And then in December 1938, in Germany, came the fateful discovery by Otto Hahn and Fritz Strassmann that sometimes when a neutron hits a uranium nucleus, the element barium with an atomic number about one half of uranium is formed. (Uranium has atomic number 92, meaning it has ninety-two protons; barium has atomic number 56).

Hahn conveyed his and Strassmann's findings to his old collaborator, Lise Meitner, who, being Jewish, had been forced earlier to leave Germany and was now living in Sweden, where she was joined for a time by her nephew, Otto Frisch, also a physicist and working in Copenhagen with Niels Bohr. In a path-breaking letter to the journal *Nature* in February 1939, "A New Type of Nuclear Reaction," Meitner and Frisch interpreted what was happening—that sometimes when a neutron strikes a uranium nucleus, the nucleus divides into two pieces, the two repelled away from each other with tremendous energy. Meitner and Frisch calculated the energy released—two hundred *million* electron volts per reaction compared to four electron volts for a chemical reaction.*[220] They also gave a name to the phenomenon—fission, a term previously used in biology to describe cell division. As we know now, the

---

* An electron volt (ev) is a unit of energy equal to about 1.6×10^{-19} joules. So, of course, even one million electron volts is not a lot of energy. But in a chain reaction, with the number of fissions increasing exponentially, the total energy release could, as we know, be massive.

fission of 3 kg of uranium-235 or plutonium can supply one day's electricity for a medium-sized American city or create fifty kilotons of explosive force. The discovery of fission was immediately hailed as epoch making by the the *New York Times*.

When physicists in the United States, Britain, France, Germany, and Russia heard of the momentous discovery of neutron-induced fission, they immediately looked to see if in the fission event more than one neutron is emitted. If that were true, a chain reaction might be possible, though even if true, whether an atomic bomb could actually be constructed was far from clear. As it turned out, each fission does emit between two and three neutrons.

This so alarmed a few American and British scientists that they agitated for their countries to initiate research to see if a bomb was possible. A key breakthrough in understanding was made by two German-Jewish émigré scientists at Birmingham University in England, Frisch (who had moved from Denmark) and Rudolph Peierls. In March 1940, the two physicists wrote a short memorandum (here termed the F-P memorandum) outlining how a bomb could be built. The memorandum, "On the construction of a Super Bomb based on a nuclear chain reaction in Uranium," for the first time developed a plausible blueprint how to construct an atomic bomb.[221]

Natural uranium is comprised of two isotopes: 0.7 percent of natural uranium is U-235 with ninety-two protons and 143 neutrons, and 99.3 percent is U-238 with ninety-two protons and 146 neutrons. Bohr learned of fission from Frisch in January 1939 as he was about to sail for America, and shortly after arriving in Princeton, he and John Wheeler, a Princeton physicist, worked out that it was the lighter and rarer isotope, U-235, that was most likely to fission when it absorbs a neutron.

The F-P memorandum took off from this insight by Bohr and Wheeler, positing that a bomb could be built using uranium highly enriched in the isotope U-235. Since the U-235 and U-238 isotopes are chemically identical, separating the isotopes would be difficult—it would have to rely on processes that exploited the very slight mass differences between the two isotopes. The memorandum, however, argued that enrichment is possible and suggested ways in which it could be accomplished. They calculated the critical mass of uranium—that is, the mass of uranium that could sustain an explosive chain reaction—to be about half a kilogram. They imagined what we now consider a gun-type weapon in which one subcritical mass of uranium is shot at another subcritical mass. As it turned out, the half-kilogram critical mass calculated was too low by a large factor—the Hiroshima bomb utilized 64 kg of uranium enriched to 80 percent U-235. The error was due to the authors assuming a cross section for fission (the probability that a neutron would strike a U-235 nucleus and cause a fission) about three times too high. However, the error, by indicating that construction of a bomb would be less daunting than in fact it is, further increased the urgency of American and British scientists to explore the feasibility of a bomb.

In Britain, in April 1940, the authorities formed the so-called MAUD Committee to explore the implications of the F-P memorandum. The committee consisted of physicists G.P. Thomson, P.M.S. Blackett, Marcus Oliphant, James Chadwick, and John Cockcroft, four of them already or soon-to-be Nobel Prize winners.[*] The other coauthor, Oliphant, we met in chapter 4; he was chair of the Physics Department at Birmingham University, where two young scientists working in the department invented the cavity magnetron, critical to the development of microwave radar and one of the factors that turned the Battle of the Atlantic against German U-boats in the Allies' favor.

In the first months of 1941, the committee completed a report, *Report by MAUD Committee on the Use of Uranium for a Bomb*, strongly supporting further work to see if a bomb could be developed, and

---

[*] Chadwick won the Nobel Prize in 1935 for is discovery of the neutron; Cockcroft in 1951 for work in splitting the atom; Thomson in 1937 for work demonstrating the wave character of electrons; and Blackett in 1948 for his investigation of cosmic rays.

sent the report to the United States.[222] The crux of the memorandum came to this:

> We have now reached the conclusion that it will be possible to make an effective uranium bomb which, containing some 25 lbs of active material, would be equivalent as regards destructive effect to 1,800 tons of T.N.T. and would also release large quantities of radioactive substance, which would make places near to where the bomb exploded dangerous to human life for a long period. ...
>
> (i)   The committee considers that the scheme for a uranium bomb is practicable and likely to lead to decisive results in the war.
> (ii) It recommends that this work be continued on the highest priority and on the increasing scale necessary to obtain the weapon in the shortest possible time.
> (iii) That the present collaboration with America should be continued and extended especially in the region of experimental work.[223]

By early 1941, scientists in the United States became aware of another possible route to a nuclear weapon other than the one charted by the F-P memorandum. Already, over a year earlier, scientists at several locations in the United States and abroad had suspected that when a neutron is absorbed by a U-238 nucleus, a new isotope with atomic number 94 is formed by the radioactive decay of the short-lived isotope, U-239. (See figure 7.1.) U-239 decays into a new element with atomic number 93, and this element decays into the element with atomic number 94. By early 1940, Glen Seaborg at Berkeley had been able to isolate in miniscule amounts the new element 94. The new elements later were named, naturally enough given that element 92 was uranium, neptunium for element 93 and plutonium for element 94.

That plutonium-239 can undergo fission was confirmed in the spring of 1940 shortly after the isotope was first isolated. Thus, in principle, it was understood that a bomb might be made either using a uranium core or a plutonium core. As described below, the bomb detonated over Hiroshima was a uranium bomb; the one used on Nagasaki was a plutonium bomb. The plutonium bomb, for reasons to be discussed later, was more complex, and it was the plutonium design that was first tested in the New Mexico desert in July 1945.

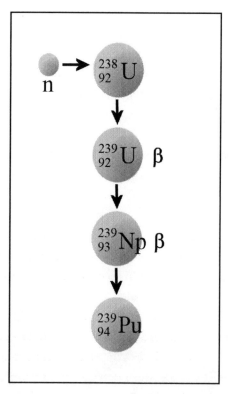

Fig. 7.1 Plutonium Production in a Nuclear Reactor (Carol Feiveson)

Leo Szilard, the Hungarian physicist who as noted was the first to conceive of a chain reaction, was deeply alarmed. Szilard, working for a time in Princeton, in August 1939 travelled to Long Island where Albert Einstein, the world's most renowned physicist, was vacationing, and there helped draft a letter that Einstein signed and sent to President Roosevelt. The key part of the letter, delivered to Roosevelt confidant, Alexander Sachs, August 15, 1939, was as follows:

> In the course of the last four months it has been made probable—through the work of Joliot in France as well as Fermi and Szilard in America—that it may become possible to set up a nuclear chain reaction in a large mass of uranium, by which vast amounts of power and large quantities of new radium-like elements would be generated. Now it appears almost certain that this could be achieved in the immediate future.
>
> This new phenomenon would also lead to the construction of bombs, and it is conceivable—though much less certain—that extremely powerful bombs of a new type may thus be constructed. ...
>
> In view of this situation you may think it desirable to have some permanent contact maintained between the Administration and the group of physicists working on chain reactions in America. ...[224]

Despite this initiative by Szilard and Einstein, the United States did little for almost two years. Indeed, when the MAUD report was sent to the United States in spring 1941, Lyman Briggs, the head of the American Uranium Committee (the committee established after the Szilard-Einstein letter got to Roosevelt), simply locked it into a safe—the report got buried. Matters got moving only when one of the authors of the MAUD report, Mark Oliphant, came over to the United States and convinced key American scientists of the urgency of the issues raised by the report. In October 1941, Vannevar Bush, the director of the newly formed Office of Scientific Research and Development (OSRD), carried the MAUD report to the president, whose support now at last galvanized the American nuclear program, soon to be termed the Manhattan Project. Shortly afterward, President Roosevelt sent a message to Prime Minister Churchill suggesting that the United States and Britain share information on matters of atomic energy, which was in fact done during the war.

The Manhattan Project

The atomic work was put under the overall supervision of the Army Corps of Engineers, which had experience in overseeing large construction projects. Initially, it was run out of the Manhattan District of the Corps—hence the origin of the name for the atomic project. In September 1942, General Lester Groves assumed command of the project.

The key tasks of the Manhattan Project were several. One was to build a reactor that could achieve a chain reaction. This was done by a team at the University of Chicago under the direction of the great Italian physicist Enrico Fermi. The chain reaction was achieved in December 1942. Secondly, efforts were mounted to produce enough fissile material for a bomb—highly enriched uranium (HEU) and plutonium. A bomb must include at least one of these materials. Neither fissile material existed in nature, and it would take a herculean effort to produce sufficient material for even one bomb in time to affect the outcome of the war. HEU was produced at Oak Ridge, Tennessee, and plutonium in large reactors built at Hanford, Washington. The work to design a bomb was done at Los Alamos, New Mexico, under the inspired direction of J. Robert Oppenheimer.

Overall, the Manhattan Project employed some 130,000 people and cost nearly $2 billion ($27 billion in 2016 dollars). It took place at over thirty sites across the United States, Britain, and Canada.[225]

Fermi Reactor and the Production of Plutonium

In the course of 1941, various experiments made it clear that the U-235 isotope could fission when absorbing both a fast neutron—that is one not slowed down after being emitted from a fission event—or a slow neutron—one slowed to thermal energy by bouncing off light nuclei. In a mass of natural or slightly enriched uranium, a chain reaction cannot be sustained by fast neutrons because the more prevalent U-238 isotope will absorb enough neutrons without fissioning to dampen any chain reaction. With slow neutrons, however, the probability of a neutron causing a U-235 fission before the neutron gets captured by a U-238 nucleus rises dramatically.

In a bomb, there has to be an explosive release of energy, so, in the core of U-235 or plutonium, the chain reaction therefore is carried by neutrons emerging from a fission event at high speeds, "fast" neutrons. As the F-P memorandum made clear, such a chain reaction requires the uranium to be highly enriched in U-235. However, if the neutrons are slowed, a chain reaction can be achieved in a mass of uranium only slightly enriched in U-235, or even in natural uranium, where the U-235 fraction is only 0.7 percent. This could be done by embedding the uranium in a matrix of light molecules that would slow but not absorb too many of the neutrons. The light material is termed a neutron "moderator."

The scientists quickly identified two candidates for a moderator: water and graphite (carbon). For natural uranium fuel, it turned out that ordinary water would not work because the hydrogen in the H_2O molecules would absorb enough neutrons to damp the chain reaction. So-called heavy water, D_2O, would have to be employed, where D is deuterium, hydrogen composed of one proton but, unlike ordinary hydrogen, also one neutron. Because of the neutron, deuterium has a lower probability of absorbing another neutron. Heavy water comprises a small fraction of seawater but can be concentrated by various painstaking isotope separation approaches. Ordinary or light water can be used as moderator if the fuel is slightly enriched in U-235, to say 4–5 percent, which is the case in modern light-water power reactors. The modern Canadian reactor, the CANDU, uses heavy water as moderator and natural uranium as fuel. Graphite would work, but it has to be of high purity so that the impurities do not absorb neutrons.

One of the first tasks of the Manhattan Project was to construct a reactor—an assembly of uranium and some moderator to slow the neutrons—capable of sustaining a controlled chain reaction, not an explosive one such as would happen with a bomb. This would first of all demonstrate the possibility of a chain reaction (heretofore only a theoretical prediction) and allow measurements of neutron absorption in various materials later critical to construction of a bomb. Secondly, it would pave a path to the production of the artificial element, plutonium, which as noted is generated in a reactor by the absorption of a neutron by the U-238 isotope.

Throughout 1941, a team under the direction of Enrico Fermi at Columbia University had been working on a uranium-graphite matrix with the goal of producing at the end a slow-neutron chain reaction. Other work exploring the chain reaction and also work on plutonium chemistry was going on elsewhere, and the scientists overseeing the nuclear efforts realized the value of placing all the reactor and plutonium-related work at one location. Columbia, the University of California at Berkeley, Princeton, and the University of Chicago were all considered, and in early 1942, the University of Chicago was chosen. Fermi began planning the full-scale chain-reacting pile in May 1942 in the squash courts of Stagg Field at the university.[226] Fermi's team included Eugene Wigner, a professor of physics at Princeton and a future Nobel Prize recipient, and Leo Szilard. The team's choice of moderator was graphite.

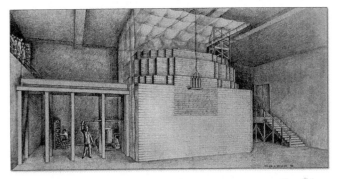

Fig. 7.2 CP-1 Fermi Reactor. The reactor went critical on December 2, 1942 under the squash courts at the University of Chicago. (Courtesy of Argonne National Laboratory)

The work proceeded diligently, day by day, with layers of uranium and graphite being laid. Instead of a sphere as initially planned, as described by Richard Rhodes, "the pile would take the form of a doorknob as big as a two-car garage, a flattened rotational ellipsoid 25 feet wide at the equator and 20 feet high from pole to pole."[227] The pile, as it waited to produce the world's first sustaining chain reaction, contained 771,000 pounds of graphite, 80,590 pounds of uranium oxide, and 12,400 pounds of uranium metal.[228] Control rods, consisting of boron, a strong neutron absorber, were interspersed throughout the matrix, assuring that the neutron multiplication could be controlled. On December 2, 1942, as the control rods were removed one by one, the pile went "critical" (i.e., the chain reaction became self-sustaining). At that point, its neutron intensity was doubling every two minutes. "Left uncontrolled for an hour and a half, that rate of increase would have carried it to a million kilowatts. Long before so extreme a runaway it would have killed anyone left in the room and melted down."[229]

Arthur Compton, another Nobel physicist, was in charge of the

University of Chicago Metallurgical Lab and called James Conant who was working in Washington. Conant, the president of Harvard and recently appointed director of the National Research Council, had been active in the formulation of science policy, including on atomic energy. In an improvised dialogue, Compton informed Conant, "You will be interested to know that the Italian navigator has just landed in the new world." "Is that so?" replied Conant. "Were the natives friendly?" "Everyone landed safe and happy," replied Compton.[230]

Plutonium Production

The Fermi reactor work led directly to the monumental task of building far larger reactors to produce plutonium. The place chosen by the Manhattan Project was a site near Hanford, Washington, on the banks of the Columbia River. Oak Ridge, Tennessee, was considered briefly, but Groves worried that if there was some kind of explosion of the reactor, there would be grave danger of massive amounts of radioactivity being released and wafted to downwind populations. The Hanford site was far more remote and sparsely populated.

In the design of the reactor, the moderator chosen was again graphite. The reactors would be releasing so much fission energy that they would have to be cooled. Helium gas was considered at one point, but eventually the reactor designers settled on water.

Three reactors were put under construction, the so-called B, D, and F reactors. Construction on the B reactor began in August 1943, and the reactor went critical in September 1944; the D reactor went critical in December 1944; and the F reactor in February 1945. Each was roughly a ten-meter cube of graphite with over two thousand channels holding the uranium fuel slugs. Water was sent through the channels for cooling. Each reactor had a design output at full power of 250 megawatts thermal heat. The plutonium production rate was about 0.8 gram of plutonium per megawatt-day. This meant that once in full operation, each reactor could produce two hundred grams of plutonium per day, or one kilogram every five days. With a core mass of 6 kg (the amount in the Trinity and Nagasaki bombs), at full operation, each reactor could produce enough plutonium for one core per month.

Along with the reactors, the Manhattan Project also included the building of three reprocessing plants (called canyons), also located near Hanford. These plants were used to chemically separate the plutonium from the uranium and highly radioactive fission products remotely behind very heavy shielding. By April 1945, the Hanford complex was sending a shipment of plutonium to Los Alamos every five days.

HEU Production

Fig. 7.3 The K-25 Gaseous Diffusion Uranium Enrichment Plant at Oak Ridge (Courtesy of Oak Ridge National Laboratory)

As noted, a uranium bomb requires uranium highly enriched in the isotope U-235. The Hiroshima bomb used 80 percent enriched uranium (and modern bombs use highly enriched uranium [HEU] containing over 90 percent U-235). In any enrichment process, the uranium has first to be converted to a chemical form suitable for the enrichment process—for example, uranium hexafluoride, which is a gas at room temperature. To produce uranium enriched in U-235 requires exploiting the slight mass difference between U-235 and U-238. In any enrichment facility, the feed stream, often but not always natural uranium, is split into two streams: a product stream enriched in U-235 and a waste or tails stream depleted in U-235.

Today, most enrichment is done by gas centrifuges, rapidly spinning cylinders where the uranium is pressed toward the outer wall with more than one hundred thousand times the force of gravity. The molecules containing the heavier U-238 atoms concentrate more toward the wall relative to the molecules containing the lighter isotope, U-235. An axial circulation of the gas is induced with the slightly enriched product emerging from one end of the centrifuge. This process is then repeated in a cascade of multiple stages to produce uranium enriched to a designated level.[231]

At the time of the Manhattan Project, however, gas centrifuge technology was ill understood. Instead the project focused on three other approaches—thermal diffusion, electromagnetic separation, and gaseous diffusion. Most critical were the last two.

Electromagnetic separation technology was based on the cyclotrons developed by Ernest Lawrence at the University of California at Berkley. The process introduces a beam of uranium-containing ions into a magnetic field that splits the beam into two by virtue of the fact that the paths of the electrically charged ions containing the lighter U-235 atoms are bent more by the magnetic field. Five separation units termed racetracks were constructed at the Oak Ridge site, the plant containing them named Y-12. Almost fifteen thousand tons of silver were used for the windings of the electromagnets.

Gaseous diffusion works by forcing uranium hexafluoride gas through a permeable membrane, where the lighter molecules would move through slightly more rapidly than the heavier molecules. At each stage, therefore, the gas on the far side of the membrane would be slightly enriched in U-235. At Oak Ridge, the Manhattan Project constructed a giant plant containing a thousand-fold stages, the plant given the code name of K-25. The plant, which commenced operation in February 1945, was four stories high and half a mile long. It consumed a very large amount of electricity – almost 300,000 KW at peak.

Ultimately, all three isotope separation processes were used. Thermal diffusion enriched natural uranium (0.7 percent U-235) to about 1 percent U-235. The 1 percent uranium was then fed to the gaseous diffusion plant, which enriched the uranium to 23 percent U-235, and this enriched product was fed to the electromagnetic separation apparatus, which produced uranium enriched to over 80 percent U-235. Sixty-four kilograms of this uranium was sent to Los Alamos in the late summer for construction of the Hiroshima bomb.

Los Alamos

The tasks confronting scientists working to design an atomic bomb were many and daunting. Among them were to calculate precisely the critical masses of HEU and plutonium; to understand the complex hydrodynamics of an exploding mass of fissile material; to devise an initiator that would start the chain reaction at the optimum moment of super-criticality; and to design carefully and precisely a way to bring a subcritical mass of fissile material into a critical assembly in a practical bomb.

To attack these myriad problems confronting the project,

Oppenheimer and Groves decided to bring together scientists and engineers from all over the country at a new lab at a remote and secluded location. The place chosen was at Los Alamos, New Mexico, an area that Oppenheimer knew and loved from many visits there in the past. The team assembled included many scientists who had already won or were soon to win Nobel prizes. These included Hans Bethe, director of the theoretical division; Enrico Fermi, who joined the Los Alamos group after his work at Chicago; Isidor Rabi, who was splitting time between Los Alamos and the radar work at the Radiation Laboratory in Cambridge; and younger scientists, such as Richard Feynman.

All the tasks initially conceived were successfully achieved. By early 1945, the Los Alamos group was confident that it could build a gun-type weapon using enriched uranium, so confident indeed that the scientists did not consider it necessary to test the weapon before its actual use. However, a still more daunting task emerged in 1944 when it was realized that the isotope, plutonium-240, which is produced in a reactor along with the plutonium-239, by non-fission absorption of a neutron by plutonium-239, fissions spontaneously, emitting neutrons. That meant that even with a relatively small amount of plutonium-240, there would be a high probability in a gun-device that the chain reaction would start prematurely as soon as the assembly achieved criticality and that the mass would blow itself apart before a significant fraction of the plutonium could fission. This meant that the gun assembly could not work with plutonium. Some new form of assembly would have to be found.

The novel idea initially put forward by Seth Neddermeyer, a young physicist trained at Cal Tech, was to construct an "implosion" device to squeeze a sphere of plutonium to a more dense state where the plutonium nuclei would be closer together, thus creating a supercritical mass. Such implosion would be produced by surrounding the plutonium sphere by lenses of chemical explosives that would produce converging shockwaves. Ultimately, under the direction of George Kistiakowsky, a Harvard chemist of distinction, the Los Alamos group developed such a lens system. The implosion alternative could achieve a supercritical mass in one-tenth to one-hundredth the time as a gun-type device. See box.

The German Nuclear Program

What most propelled the Manhattan Project was the fear that the Germans were working on atomic weapons. Fission was first discovered in Germany, and though many of the best German scientists were Jewish and had been driven out of the country, many outstanding scientists remained. Germany had access to the uranium-oxide stored by Union-Miniere in Belgium and potentially to thousands of tons of uranium ore in the Belgian Congo. They also had access to the Norwegian plant at Vemork, producing, among other products, heavy water.

As Fermi had in the United States, the Germans sought to achieve a chain reaction using uranium and a moderator to slow the neutrons. Some experiments in 1940 convinced the German scientists that graphite would not work as a moderator, and they focused on heavy water as the most suitable moderator. The atomic research was gathered under the direction of Werner Heisenberg, who had won a Nobel Prize for his path-breaking work on quantum mechanics. Heisenberg was not a Nazi, and he had defended "Jewish physics" against attacks on Einstein and others by the Nazis. But he was a German nationalist and chose to remain in Germany.

During 1941, Heisenberg and collaborators had made some progress in measuring critical masses and in construction of a prototype of a uranium pile. They also understood by September that, in principle, it would be possible to breed the fissile element 94 in a reactor. So it was that after the war, Heisenberg wrote, "It was from September 1941 that we saw an open road ahead of us, leading to an atomic bomb."[232]

Copenhagen. In October 1941, Heisenberg travelled to German-occupied Copenhagen, in part to see his old friend and mentor, Niels Bohr. In the 1920s, Bohr and Heisenberg, then only in his twenties, working together had made tremendous contributions to the theory of quantum mechanics. Though Bohr refused to undertake any work with German scientists, he greeted his old colleague warmly. But in a conversation during a long evening walk, Heisenberg said something that shocked Bohr. Heisenberg and Bohr have given different accounts on what was said—Heisenberg explaining after the war that when he mentioned to Bohr that to develop an atomic bomb would require a terrific technical effort, Bohr took this to mean that Germany had made great progress, which was not at all the case and not what Heisenberg wished to convey. At any rate, Bohr was greatly alarmed and shared his concerns with scientists in the Manhattan Project.[233] The dramatic meeting is examined in Michael Frayn's engrossing play, *Copenhagen.*

In the event, however, it turned out that the Germans made little progress toward a bomb, though this did not become clear to the Allies until 1945, as related below.

Vemork Heavy Water Plant. Concern of what the Germans might be up to led to one of the most dramatic commando raids of the war. As noted, to achieve a chain reaction in a uranium reactor requires a moderator to slow the fission neutrons. While Fermi used graphite as the moderator for the Chicago pile, it was well understood by scientists that heavy water also could be used. And the world's main site for heavy water production was in German-controlled Norway at a difficult-to-bomb mountain enclave near the town of Vemork. Indeed, weeks before the war in the West, in February 1940, the Norwegians and the French contrived in a dramatic action to remove canisters of heavy water from Vemork and eventually to ship them to Britain.[234] But after the Germans occupied Norway, the production of heavy water accelerated. The Allies were determined to attack this site.

In November 1942, four Norwegian commandoes, located in Britain, parachuted into the mountain region near Vemork to prepare the way for a glider attack. But the gliders crashed in bad weather and were discovered by the Germans. All the survivors of the attack were executed the same day. The Allies tried again. On February 6, 1943, six Norwegians native to the region and trained as Special Forces parachuted onto a frozen lake thirty miles northwest of Vemork. The men were equipped with skis, supplies, shortwave radio, and sets of plastic explosives. They rendezvoused some days later with the four Norwegians who had parachuted in on November of the year before and who had hidden out in the mountains for three months.

With information supplied by Lief Tronstad, one of the chief designers of the Vemork plant and now responsible in the Norwegian High Command in London for intelligence and sabotage, the group set out on skis February 27, well armed, and organized into a covering party and a demolition party. Crossing a gorge and frozen lake, the invaders took the plant completely by surprise, destroyed most of the stored heavy water, and damaged the plant. The entire invading party escaped.[235]

This was not the end of the story, however. The Germans rebuilt the plant and by early 1944 had produced a large quantity of heavy water. Alerted by insider information, in February, word came to the Allies that thirty-nine drums of heavy water were to be transported under guard to Germany in a week or two. The responsibility to find a way to attack the transport was now in the hands of Knut Haukelid, one of the group that had attacked Vemork a year earlier, and now the only trained commando in the area. The transportation route had several stages, and Haukelid decided to focus on a ferry crossing of Lake Tinnsjo. Haukelid and Rolf Sorlie, a local compatriot he had enlisted, slipped onto the ferry, planted explosives, and set them to be timed to explode when the ferry was in the deepest part of the lake—hoping that all or most of the innocent travelers aboard the ferry could survive. The bombs detonated as planned, and the drums of heavy water sank. Twenty-six passengers lost their lives. In the words of Richard Rhodes, "The race to the bomb, such as it was, ended for Germany on a mountain lake in Norway on a cold Sunday morning in February 1944."[236]

Alsos and Farm Hall. The lack of progress by the Germans finally became clear to the Allies after D-Day and the sweep of Allied armies across France into Germany. In late 1943, General Groves set up an intelligence unit, code-named Alsos, to follow the Allied armies as they advanced toF try to determine what the Germans were doing with atomic energy. The overall director was Lt. Colonel Boris Pash, fluent in Russian; the technical director of Alsos was Samuel Goudsmit, a Jewish-Dutch physicist, who had been working at the Radiation Laboratory in Cambridge, Massachusetts.

Uncovering various German documents, the Alsos group became aware by the spring of 1945 that the Germans were far behind the Allies in atomic research. The group also located and took control of most of the uranium ore that the Germans had confiscated when they invaded Belgium in 1940. And it became even more clear how far the Germans were behind the Allies when the key German scientists, including Heisenberg and Hahn, the discoverer of fission, were rounded up in April.

The German scientists were interred in Britain at Farm Hall, a country house north of Cambridge. Their conversations were monitored and recorded by hidden microphones. When they heard by radio of the bombing of Hiroshima, they were at first astounded; the little work they had done had convinced them that to construct a bomb by 1945 was impossible. But as they pondered more, they did come to realize more or less how the Allies had done it.

Trinity

By the summer of 1945, the Los Alamos scientists were so confident that the gun-type uranium weapon they had designed would work that no test was required. Much of their work during the past year had been to develop an implosion weapon that could work with plutonium as the fissile core. This complex design needed to be tested, and now enough plutonium was being delivered to Los Alamos to allow a test by the middle of July. Such a test, code-named Trinity, would of course also be the first atomic bomb explosion ever and thus a dramatic and watershed moment in human history.

The place chosen for Trinity was a remote valley in New Mexico, about two hundred miles south of Los Alamos, known from Spanish times as the Jornado del Muerto, the Journey of Death. The implosion weapon contained about six kilograms of plutonium, which was delivered to the Laboratory in early July. The time designated for the test was before dawn on Monday, July 16, 1945.

During the night before, the weapon—weighing roughly five metric tons—was hoisted up a tower, and with a lightning storm raging around the area, the final connections were made by the scientists. Oppenheimer, Groves, and others stationed themselves about five miles from ground zero. Hans Bethe, Ernest Lawrence, Edward Teller, and others were at Campania Hill, twenty miles from ground zero. Several of the scientists had taken bets on how large an explosion it would be. Teller guessed forty-five kilotons, Bethe eight kilotons, Oppenheimer thought about three hundred tons; Rabi guessed closest to the actual yield, about eighteen kilotons of TNT equivalent.

Richard Rhodes describes the scene: After some delays, the bomb was scheduled to be detonated at 5:30 a.m., just before Dawn. The countdown began some minutes earlier, with the tension almost unbearable. To those waiting, the final minute seemed an eternity. The bomb went off at 5:30 a.m. For those who witnessed this first atomic explosion, the experience was shattering and awe inspiring. As Rabi wrote,

> "Those ten seconds [before detonation] were the longest ten seconds that I had ever experienced. Suddenly there was an enormous flash of light, the brightest light I have ever seen or that I think anyone has ever seen. It blasted, it pounced, it bored its way right through you. … Finally it was over, diminishing, and we looked toward the place where the bomb had been: there was an enormous ball of fire which grew and grew and it rolled as it grew; it went up into the air, in yellow lashes and into scarlet and green. It looked menacing. It seemed to come toward one. A new thing had just been born; a new control; a new understanding of man, which man had acquired over nature."[237]

The Decision to Drop the Bomb

Although, as noted, the race for the bomb by the Allies was in large part galvanized by a fear that the Germans were working toward a bomb, even after the German unconditional surrender on May 8, 1945, work on the bomb continued. The possible use of the bomb now became focused on Japan.

In early May 1945, just as Germany was about to surrender, President Truman appointed an interim committee to propose how the United States should use the atomic bomb when it was ready. The committee was chaired by Secretary of War Henry Stimson and included the soon-to-be-appointed Secretary of State James Byrnes, Vannevar Bush, James Conant, and others. Stimson was then seventy-seven years old with a distinguished career in government. Richard Rhodes adds the striking note that Stimson "could remember stories his great grandmother told him of her childhood talks with George Washington."[238]

The committee created a scientific panel to provide advice from the atomic scientists. The panel was composed of Robert Oppenheimer, Enrico Fermi, Ernest Lawrence, and Arthur Compton. Meeting on June 16–17 in Los Alamos, the panel was unable to conjure up a way that the bomb could be used in a demonstration vivid enough to end the war. It concluded as follows:

> Those who advocate a purely technical demonstration would wish to outlaw the use of atomic weapons, and have feared that if we use the weapons now our position in future negotiations will be prejudiced. Others emphasize the opportunity of saving American lives by immediate military use, and believe that such use will improve the international prospects, in that they are more concerned with the prevention of war than with the elimination of this specific weapon. We find ourselves closer to these latter views; we can propose no technical demonstration likely to bring an end to the war; we see no acceptable alternative to direct military use.[239]

The scientists' findings were made before the dramatic test of the first atomic bomb in the New Mexico desert on July 16, 1945. All who witnessed the test were awed by what they saw. One wonders if the report of the scientific panel had come after the test whether a demonstration explosion would have appeared more worthy of consideration.

The interim committee under Stimson came to a similar

conclusion. And so the die was cast for the use of the first atomic bombs against targets in Japan unless Japan agreed to the conditions set forth by the Allies in the so-called Potsdam declaration of July 26, designed to give the Japanese an opportunity to end the war. The declaration, in the names of the president of the United States, the president of the National Government of the Republic of China, and the prime minister of Great Britain, stated the following:

> Following are our terms. We will not deviate from them. There are no alternatives. We shall brook no delay.
>
> There must be eliminated for all time the authority and influence of those who have deceived and misled the people of Japan into embarking on world conquest, for we insist that a new order of peace, security and justice will be impossible until irresponsible militarism is driven from the world.
>
> Until such a new order is established and until there is convincing proof that Japan's war-making power is destroyed, points in Japanese territory to be designated by the Allies shall be occupied to secure the achievement of the basic objectives we are here setting forth.
>
> We do not intend that the Japanese shall be enslaved as a race or destroyed as a nation, but stern justice shall be meted out to all war criminals, including those who have visited cruelties upon our prisoners. The Japanese Government shall remove all obstacles to the revival and strengthening of democratic tendencies among the Japanese people. Freedom of speech, of religion, and of thought, as well as respect for the fundamental human rights shall be established.

The occupying forces of the Allies shall be withdrawn from Japan as soon as these objectives have been accomplished and there has been established in accordance with the freely expressed will of the Japanese people a peacefully inclined and responsible government.

We call upon the government of Japan to proclaim now the unconditional surrender of all Japanese armed forces, and to provide proper and adequate assurances of their good faith in such action. The alternative for Japan is prompt and utter destruction.[240]

The declaration was silent on the future of the Japanese emperor. Perhaps had the Allies been explicit that Japan could keep the emperor (as they did make implicitly just before the Japanese surrendered on August 11), the war could have been ended without the atomic bombing of two Japanese cities. But this is one of those sad what-might-have-beens that can never be proven one way or the other.

The Bombing of Hiroshima and Nagasaki

On August 6, 1945, one B-29 bomber, the Enola Gay, accompanied by two other B-29s equipped with cameras and scientific equipment for measuring the effects of the explosion, took off from the island of Tinian and flew toward the city of Hiroshima. At 8:10 a.m. Hiroshima time, the Enola Gay started its fateful run over the city, and at 8:15 a.m., the first atomic bomb to be used in war, a uranium bomb whose design had not been tested, was dropped. Sixty thousand were killed instantly, and many more thousands died later from radiation illness and cancer due to neutron radiation from the explosion. The city was largely destroyed.

On August 8, the Soviet Union launched an attack across the Manchurian frontier. The following day, August 9, having heard nothing from Japan, the United States dropped a plutonium bomb on the city of Nagasaki. It destroyed much of the city, killing instantly thirty-nine thousand.

The Japanese military remained adamant against surrender. But on the night after the Nagasaki bombing, the emperor summoned the Supreme Council and strongly supported accepting the terms of the Potsdam declaration, providing that the imperial house and its succession was preserved. The Allies accepted this condition, and on August 14, a military coup having failed, the Japanese surrendered. Some historians argue that Japan was near to surrender in any case, and especially so after the Soviet Union launched its attack. Perhaps this is so. But clearly the atomic bombs strengthened the position of the emperor in accepting surrender against the vehement opposition of much of the military. The formal surrender of Japan took place at Tokyo Bay on September 2, 1945.[241]

And so ended the Second World War.

An Explosive Chain Reaction

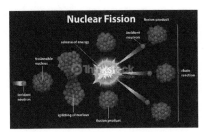

Fig. 7.4 A Fast Fission Chain Reaction

The nuclei of all elements (other than the lightest hydrogen isotope, which contains one proton and no neutrons) contain positively charged protons and neutrally charged neutrons. Electromagnetic forces, where like-charged particles repel each other (see chapter 2) would tend to drive the nucleus apart by the protons interacting with one another but are balanced by very strong attractive nuclear forces that operate at very short distances.

However, when a uranium-235 nucleus absorbs a neutron, the attractive forces are weakened, the nucleus fissions into two nuclei of medium atomic weight (for example, barium and krypton), and the two fission products repel each other with tremendous force. The fission also releases two or three neutrons, which can then cause a chain reaction in a critical mass of material.

An explosive chain reaction proceeds very rapidly, with each generation taking about one hundred millionth of a second. Eighty doublings of the neutron population in a millionth of a second could fission one kilogram of material and release an energy equivalent to eighteen thousand tons of high explosive (TNT).

Why Plutonium Cannot Be Used in a Gun-Type Weapon

Even in weapon-grade plutonium, where the Pu-239 fraction is about 93 percent, there will still be about 6 percent Pu-240. Pu-240 fissions spontaneously, emitting neutrons. For such weapon-grade plutonium, the neutron emission rate is about 64,000 neutrons per kg-second. The critical mass of the first plutonium bombs was about 6 kg, so that the total emission rate of neutrons was about 384,000 neutrons per second.

In a gun-type weapon, the maximum muzzle velocity would be less than 3,000 feet/second. If then the two subcritical masses in the gun are say one foot apart, it would take over 1/3,000 seconds for the two to reach super-criticality. But at a spontaneous fission rate of 384,000 neutrons per second, in that 1/3,000 seconds, over one hundred neutrons would be emitted, making it virtually certain that the chain reaction would be initiated well before the assembly becomes supercritical, assuring a fizzle.

In an implosion event, however, the implosion shockwave reaches the core in less than 10^{-5} seconds, roughly one hundred times quicker than in a gun-device. This could still lead to a fizzle but with a much lower probability. [See Carson Mark, *Science and Global Security* 4 (1993): 111–128.]

In an important article, Carson Mark, a Canadian physicist and who after the war was director of the theoretical division at Los Alamos, explained the implosion event in much more detail. He referred to an Oppenheimer memorandum that noted that with the Trinity implosion assembly system and the grade of plutonium employed, there was an 88 percent probability that the device would survive long enough without a chain reaction being initiated to achieve the nominal yield of 20 kt, and about 94 percent probability that the yield would be over 5 kt. As Mark shows, if the assembly system was twice as rapid, the probability of a full yield would be over 94 percent.

The importance of this analysis derives from the much later concern about whether so-called reactor-grade plutonium could be used in a bomb.

Bibliography

Feiveson, Harold, Alexander Glaser, Zia Mian, and Frank von Hippel. *Unmaking the Bomb: A Fissile Material Approach to Nuclear Disarmament and Nonproliferation*, chapter 2, "Production, Uses, and Stocks of Fissile Materials" and chapter 3, "The History of Fissile Material Production for Weapons." MIT Press, 2014.

Hartcup, Guy. *The Effect of Science on the Second World War*, chapter 10, "The Ultimate Weapon: The Atomic Bomb." Palgarave, 2003.

Olson, Lynne. *Last Hope Island*. Random House, 2017.

Rhodes, Richard. *The Making of the Atomic Bomb*. Simon and Schuster, 1986.

Film

The Day After Trinity—directed by Jon Else (1981), focusing on J. Robert Oppenheimer and the work he directed at Los Alamos.

The Heavy Water War, directed by Per-Olav Sorenson for Norway Television.

Afterword: Scientists and War

When the war ended, the Allied scientists and engineers could look back with some pride that they had contributed invaluably to victory. Radar and the development of the Spitfire and Hurricane had played a critical role in the climactic Battle of Britain; microwave radar, high-frequency direction finding, the Hedgehog antisubmarine weapon, operations research, and the development of modern aircraft carriers had turned around the Battle of the Atlantic against Nazi U-Boats; the development of navigation aids, the proximity fuse, and, above all, the development of the P-51 Mustang interceptor had dramatically contributed to victory in the air; the development of a suite of amphibious craft and various counter-radar technologies had played a vital role in the invasion of the European continent; the Russian development of the T-34 tank, the Katyusha rocket, and other weapons were vital innovations on the Eastern Front; and cryptographers at Bletchley Court by breaking the German Enigma impacted over the entire European and Mediterranean theaters of operation.

In the Pacific theater as well, advances in Allied technology—modern amphibious craft, new weapons such as flame-throwers, fast aircraft carriers, breakthroughs in cryptography, the Hellcat fighter, and the remarkable B-29 super-fortress among them—were all critical to victory. In all theaters of war, advances in medicine—the development of sulpha drugs, penicillin, antimalarials, insecticides, and other—saved countless lives. A myriad of technical innovations in industrial production, in the United States especially, were central to the remarkable surge of weapons production by the Allies.

And, most dramatic of all, despite that fission was first discovered in Germany, it was the Allied scientists who developed the atomic bomb.

Overall, though the Germans (and at the start of the war, the Japanese also) had impressive achievements in weapons design—most notably, by the Germans, in the development of sophisticated tanks, the V-1 unmanned bomber, the V-2 rocket, and the Me-262 jet—these achievements were far overshadowed by the scientific innovations of the Allies. While the Allies were able to forge close cooperation among scientists and military officers, the Germans and Japanese never were.

The civilian legacies in the postwar era of the scientific advances made during the war were of course prodigious—in radar, in aircraft design, in rocket technology, in computers, in medicine, in industrial design, and in atomic power.

The military legacies were also immense—above all in the development of nuclear weapons and long-range missiles. Also striking has been the determination of governments to mobilize their scientific resources for weapons purposes, leading in the United States, for example, to the establishment of weapon laboratories hosting thousands of scientists and technical experts.

However, at the same time, the war taught scientists in all the Allied countries to get involved in public policy. In Russia, for example, Andrei Sakharov played a critical role in challenging Soviet weapons policy in the postwar era. In the United States, scientists mobilized to ensure that atomic energy would come under civilian authority, and the formation of the Federation of Atomic Scientists (soon to be rebranded the Federation of American Scientists) assured that independent scientists would have an active role in addressing US defense policy, especially policies affecting nuclear weapons.

While the legacies of World War II are of unprecedented promise and peril and will demand unstinting attention by scientists and statesmen in the future, nevertheless we should be grateful that Allied scientists played their part in defeating in World War II, one of the greatest scourges the world has ever faced.

Endnotes

Chapter 1

1   Williamson Murray and Alan Millett, *A War To Be Won: Fighting the Second World War*, 3.

2   Antony Beevor, *The Second World War*, 3.

3   Neville Chamberlain speech, September 27, 1938.

4   Winston Churchill speech in House of Commons, October 5, 1938.

5   Murray, 16–17.

6   Gary Hess, *The United States at War*, 16.

7   Ian Kershaw, *Fateful Choices*, 107.

8   Kershaw, 108.

9   Planners in the Japanese navy general staff concluded in 1940 that "we are not very confident of our capacity for endurance" in a protracted war with the United States. Yet, basing all their hopes on a decisive blow in a short conflict, they continued to reckon with and plan for war, 'for the survival of the empire whether we like it or not'" [Kershaw, 118].

10 Kershaw, 123.

11 Beevor, 249.

12 Murray, 65–66.

13 Kershaw, 33.

14 Roosevelt speech, June 11, 1940.

15 Richard Evans, *The Third Reich at War*, 178–179.

16 Kershaw, 247.

17 Kershaw, 284–290.

18 Murray, 142.

19 Murray, 133.

20 Murray, 141.

21 Murray, 115.

22 Evans, 185; Beevor, 417.

23 Lynne Olson, *Those Angry Days*, 132–134, 243–246.

24 Evans, 486.

25 Paul Kennedy, *Engineers of Victory*, 184–192.

26 Richard Overy, *Why the Allies Won*, 243.

27 Murray, 270.

28 Murray, 272.

29 This is a story told in Ben McIntyre, *Operation Mincemeat*.

30 Craig Symonds, *The Battle of Midway*.

31 Overy, *Why the Allies Won*, 52.

32 Kennedy, 323–328.

33 Kennedy 328–333.

34 Guy Hartcup, *The Effect of Science on the Second World War*, 123–130.

35 In January 1942, the administration ordered the automobile industry to cease all production of civilian cars and trucks. The half million or so cars in company inventories and still on assembly lines were not to be sold through dealers but rationed out to high-priority users such as doctors and police.

36 The bomber was the B-24 Liberator [Klein, 675].

37 Maury Klein, *A Call to Arms*, 304–305, 515–518, 675.

38 Max Hastings, *All Hell Broke Loose*, 480; Overy, *The Bombers and the Bombed*.

39 The US strategic bombing survey estimated that the industrial effort and resources devoted to these revenge weapons equaled production of twenty-four thousand fighter aircraft.

40 Quoted in Rick Atkinson, *The Guns at Last Light*, 179.

41 Beevor, 729–730.

42 Murray, 483.

Chapter 2

43 Lynne Olson, *Last Hope Island*.

44 Len Deighton, *Fighter: The True Story of the Battle of Britain*, 117.

45 Robert Buderi, *The Invention that Changed the World*, 52.

46 Stanley Baldwin, November 10, 1932.

47 Buderi, 54.

48 Robert Watson-Watt, "Detection and Location of Aircraft by Radio Methods," memorandum, February 12, 1935.

49 Guy Hartcup, *The Effect of Science on the Second World War*, 14.

50 Watson-Watt. He wrote in memo that for a plane about 8.5 km distant, a field of fourteen millivolts per meter would be established at plane. If plane is 50 m, then total voltage would be about seven hundred millivolts. This would produce in wing about 1.5 milliamperes—all this per ampere in the sending aerial. Reflected field returned would be about twenty microvolts.

51 Buderi, 58.

52 Deighton, 118.

53 Buderi, 61.

54 Hartcup, 19.

55 Richard Feynman, *Lectures in Physics*, II, I-3.

56 Feynman, II, I-11.

57 "We may think of E and B as giving the forces that would be experienced at the time t by a charge located at some point in space, with the condition that placing the charge there did not disturb the positions or motions of all the other charges responsible for the fields" [Feynman, II, I-3].

58 Frederick E. Terman, *Electronic and Radio Engineering*, McGraw-Hill, 1955. "The strength of a radio wave is measured in terms of the voltage produced in space by the electric field of the wave, usually expressed in microvolts per meter. Since the actual stress produced at any point by an alternating wave varies sinusoidaly from instant to instant, it is customary to consider the intensity of such a wave to be the effective value of the stress, which is 0.707 times the maximum stress ... ."

59 Terman, 3.

60 Terman, 1016 ff.

61 Terman, 5.

62 Terman, 239.

63 Terman, 1018: "It is customary to describe the target in terms of an equivalent cross section S such that if the total power contained in a section of the incident wave front having the area S were radiated by an isotropic radiator located at the target, the strength of the wave thereby reaching the receiving antenna would be the same as the strength of the actual echo produced by the target."

64 Stephen Phelps, *The Tizard Mission*, photos after p. 120.

65 Overy, *The Battle of Britain*, 46.

66 Deighton, 129.

67 Deighton, 130.

68 Deighton, 131.

69 "Yet for most of the fighters, the colored counters on the plotting tables were no more than 4 minutes—about 15 miles—behind events. It proved good enough" [Deighton, 136–137].

70 The BF-109 was designed by Willy Emil Messerschmitt; the Hurricane was designed by Sidney Camm. German aircraft also included the Messerschmitt 110, a two-engine fighter but much less formidable than the B-109.

71 PV-12 stands for private venture, twelve cylinder. Private venture because the Merlin was developed by Rolls-Royce without government funding.

72 G. Geoffrey Smith, *Frederick Henry Royce: An Outline of His Engineering Achievement* (Longmans Green and Co., 1945).

73 Deighton, 112.

74 Overy, *The Battle of Britain*, 34–38.

75 Overy, 55.

76 Deighton, 55.

77 Deighton, 169–170.

78 Deighton, 218–219.

79 Deighton, 229.

80 Deighton, 244.

81 Deighton, 267; also see R.V. Jones, *Most Secret War* (Hamish-Hamilton, 1978), chapters 16–17.

82 Deighton, 290.

83 Deighton 307–308.

84 A.J.P. Taylor, Introduction, *Fighter*, xxiv.

85 Max Hastings, *All Hell Broke Loose*, 81.

86 Deighton, 339.

Chapter 3

87 Number is $26!/(14!6!2^6)$. The plugboard adds tremendously to the number of possibilities but without scramblers could be attacked by frequency methods, since the plugboard alone is a monoalphabetic cipher. $26!/14! = 26^*25^*...^*15 =$ number for six plugboard switches of two letters. 6! captures that we don't care where say AB appears in string of letters. 2^6 captures idea that say A-B is same as B-A].

88 Simon Singh, *The Code Book*, 146–160; see also Andrew Hodges, *Alan Turing: The Enigma*, 215–222.

89 Stephen Budiansky, *Battle of Wits*, 73.

90 Budiansky, *Battle of Wits*, 106–109.

91 Singh, 155.

92 Andrew Hodges, 221–222.

93 Singh, 162.

94 Singh, 160.

95 Lynne Olson, *Last Hope Island*, 164–165. For a period, the Polish cryptographers were in southern France and in communication with Bletchley.

96 Budiansky, *Battle of Wits*, 115; Hodges, 123–130.

97 Hodges, 434–435.

98 Budiansky, *Battle of Wits*, 125.

99 Singh, 170–178.

100 Hodges, 229–230.

101 Hodges, 231.

102 Sinclair McKay, *The Secret Lives of Codebreakers*, chapters 15, 19.

103 Singh, *Codebook*, 174.

104 Budiansky, *Battle of Wits*, 207.

105 Budiansky, *Battle of Wits*, 286. This instead of a combat medal on the grounds that the two had died half an hour after the fighting had stopped.

106 Budiansky, *Battle of Wits*, 282–286.

107 Len Deighton, *Fighter*, 41.

108 Antony Beevor, *The Second World War*, 188–189.

109 Budiansky, *Battle of Wits*, 270–272.

110 Budiansky, *Battle of Wits*, 294.

111 Hodges, Chapter 8; Singh, 189.

112 Other Native American code talkers were also used in the war, including Lakota soldiers, though not on the scope of the Navajos.

Chapter 4

113 Winston Churchill, *Second World War, II*, 529.

114 Richard Overy, *Why the Allies Won*, 55–56.

115 Stephen Budiansky, *Battle of Wits*, 279.

116 Richard Overy, *Why the Allies Won*, 57.

117 Overy, 62.

118 Overy, 59.

119 Overy, 58.

120 Overy, 64.

121 Budiansky, *Battle of Wits*, 292.

122 Stephen Budiansky, *Blackett's War*, 242.

123 Overy, 65.

124 Budiansky, *Blackett's War*, 242.

125 The "incubator" here was a small admiralty unit called the DMWD or Department of Miscellaneous Weapons Development, fondly known as the Wheezers and Dodgers. Among the DMWD's staff was a Lieutenant-Colonel Stewart Blacker, then in his fifties but someone who had been interested in blowing things up since he was a schoolboy in Bedford. It was he who conceived the hedgehog. [Paul Kennedy, *Engineers of Victory*, 55–57.]

126 Budiansky, *Blackett's War*, 207–208.

127 Guy Hartcup, *The Effect of Science on the Second World War*, 48.

128 Hartcup, 48.

129 Antony Beevor, *The Second World War*, 438.

130 E.G. Bowen, *Radio Days*, 143.

131 Bowen, 147.

132 Buderi, 85–86.

133 Frederick Terman, *Electronic and Radio Engineering*, 689.

134 Bowen, *Radio Days*, 148.

135 James Phinney Baxter III, *Scientists against Time*, 1946.

136 Budiansky, *Blackett's War*, 205.

137 Kennedy, chapter 1.

138 Kennedy, 43.

139 Overy, 71.

140 Overy, 74.

Chapter 5

141 Sir Alan Cook, "Reginald Victor Jones," *Biographical Memoirs of Fellows of the Royal Society* 45 (November 1999): 240–254.

142 Robert Buderi, *The Invention that Changed the World*, 192–193; R.V. Jones, *Most Secret War*, 92–105.

143 Jones, 67–71; Buderi, 195.

144 Jones, 102, 127–128.

145 Richard Overy, *The Bombers and the Bombed*, 41–47: "On May 15, 1940, the cabinet finally took decision to approve a full bombing strategy against German targets where civilians might be casualties, as long as there were 'suitable military objectives.'"

146 Overy, *Bombers*, 66.

147 Overy, *Bombers*, 67.

148 Overy, *Bombers*, 68–70.

149 Overy, *Bombers*, 90–99.

150 Overy, *Bombers*, 129.

151 Jones, 275–276.

152 Jones, 276.

153 Overy, *Bombers*, 99–100; Jones, 275.

154 The strategic bombing of Japan was more directly aimed at city destruction.

155 Antony Beevor, *The Second World War*, 445.

156 Beevor 445–448.

157 Overy, *Bombers*, 104.

158 Beevor, 446.

159 Overy, *Bombers*, 141–147.

160 Overy, *Bombers*, 131, 145; Beevor, 455.

161 Beevor, 450.

162 Harris at last recognized that the effectiveness of German night defenses, as he told the Air Ministry, might soon create a situation in which loss rates "could not in the end be sustained." [Overy, *Bombers*, 183–185.]

163 Harris had promised that the bombing of Berlin would be decisive. Battle went on from August 1943 to March 1944. Harris had badly miscalculated and was finally forced to back down. Bomber Command had lost over a thousand aircraft, the majority to night fighters.

164 Overy, *Bombers*, 152–153.

165 Jones, 467; Overy, *Bombers*, 207.

166 Overy, *Bombers*, 117, 170.

167 Overy, *Bombers*, 200.

168 Overy, *Bombers*, 203.

169 Kennedy, 116 ff; David Birch, *Rolls Royce and the Mustang*, 9–10.

170 Paul Ludwig, *The Development of the P-51 Long-Range Interceptor Mustang*, 82; Birch, 9–10; Kennedy, 121-123.

171 Birch book includes a long memorandum by Thomas Hitchcock. Birch also has a note on Challier.

172 The Mustang got 3.3 miles per gallon, while the P-47 got less than 1.8. [Marshall Michel, "The P-51 Mustang: the Most Important Aircraft in History?" *Air Power History* 5.4 (Winter 2008).]

173 Kennedy, 123-126.

174 Marshall Michel, "The P-51 Mustang: the Most Important Aircraft in History?" *Air Power History* 5.4 (Winter 2008).

175 Overy, *Bombers*, 180–189.

176 Overy, *Bombers*, 191.

177 Kennedy, 131–132.

178 Overy, *Bombers*, 206.

179 Overy, *Bombers,* 209.

180 Overy, *Bombers*, 225 ff.

181 Overy, *Bombers*, 228–229.

182 Murray, 260.

183 What the continuation of the West's [indiscriminate] bombing did was to stain its reputation and "produce a moral equivalent to what the Luftwaffe had done to Warsaw, Rotterdam, and Coventry" [Kennedy, 82].

184 Michael Walzer, "World War II: Why Was This War Different," *Philosophy and Public Affairs*, 1971.

185 When the distance between the fuse and the target changes rapidly, then the phase relationship also changes rapidly.

186 Guy Hartcup, *The Effect of Science on the Second World War*, 157.

187 Murray, 333.

188 Overy, *Bombers*, 206.

189 Hartcup, 159–166.

Chapter 6

190 Williamson Murray, *A War To Be Won*, 412.

191 Chester Wilmot, *The Struggle for Europe*, 186.

192 Murray, 416.

193 Murray, 412-413; Weinberg, 686.

194 Anthony Cave Brown, *Bodyguard of Lies*, 462.

195 Brown, 473 ff.

196 Brown, 480.

197 Paul Kennedy, *Engineers of Victory*, 257.

198 Ben McIntyre, *Doublecross*, tells the story of the double agents with great flair.

199 Richard Overy, *Why the Allies Won*, 189.

200 Brown, 668.

201 Overy, *Why the Allies Won*, 191.

202 Wilmot, 220.

203 Wilmot, 194.

204 Kennedy, 270.

205 Wilmot, 219.

206 R.V. Jones, *Most Secret War*, 401.

207 Jones, 405–406.

208 Atkinson, 31.

209 Brown, 626.

210 Brown, 636.

211 Murray, 420.

212 Ramsay was also architect of the Dunkirk evacuation.

213 Brown, 639.

214 Atkinson, 24.

215 Murray, 422–425; In a violent storm on June 19, the Omaha Mulberry was destroyed.

216 Kennedy 276.

217 Murray 413.

218 Lynne Olson, *Last Hope Island*, chapter 21.

Chapter 7

219 Frederick Soddy, *Atomic Transformation*, 95; Richard Rhodes, *The Making of the Atomic Bomb*, 44. The history of fission is exceptionally well told by Rhodes's book, chapter 1.

220 An electron volt (ev) is a unit of energy equal to about 1.6×10^{-19} joules. So, of course, even one million electron volts is not a lot of energy. But in a chain reaction, with the number of fissions increasing exponentially, the total energy release could, as we know, be massive.

221 atomicarchive.com/Docs/Begin/FrischPeierls.shml.

222 The draft report was done in March 1941, the final report in June 1941.

223 atomicarchive.com/Docs/Begin/MAUD.shtml.

224 atomicarchive.com/Docs/Begin/Einstein.shmtl.

225 Wikipedia, *Manhattan Project*, January 20, 2015.

226 Rhodes, 428.

227 Rhodes, 435.

228 Rhodes, 435–436.

229 Rhodes, 440.

230 Rhodes, 442.

231 H.A. Feiveson et al., *Unmaking the Bomb*, 31.

232 Rhodes, 383.

233 Rhodes, 383–385.

234 Lynne Olson, *Last Hope Island*, 70–81.

235 Rhodes, 455–457.

236 Rhodes, 517.

237 Rhodes, 672.

238 Rhodes, 618.

239 Rhodes, 697.

240 atomicarchive.com/Docs/Hiroshima/Potsdam.shml.

241 Antony Beevor, *The Second World War*, 774–776.

Acknowledgments

I would like to thank Paul Miles, retired lecturer in history at Princeton, who first gave me the idea for my freshman seminars on scientists in World War II and who read an early draft of this book. I wish also to acknowledge my colleague Frank von Hippel, who read an early draft of this book and provided many valuable comments. I also wish to express my appreciation to all my colleagues at the Program on Science and Global Security with their abiding concern for how science impacts international affairs. I thank also William Happer for his tutorial on radar. I am also of course much indebted to the vast number of books on World War II by historians, which I have much relied upon.

I would like to thank my wife, who prepared the timeline of World War II, and my children, who read and commented on earlier drafts. They also drew six of the images included in the book.

Above all, I would like to thank my students in the freshman seminar for their class presentations and midterm and term papers, which provided me much valuable material.

Index

C

D

E

F

Iwo Jima, Battle of xvii, 28

About the Author

H. A. Feiveson retired as a senior research scientist at the Program on Science and Global Security at Princeton University—a program he co-directed for thirty years. He is the co-author of *Unmaking the Bomb: A Fissile Material Approach to Nuclear Disarmament and Nonproliferation*, published by MIT Press in 2014, and editor and co-author of *The Nuclear Turning Point: A Blueprint for Deep Cuts and De-Alerting of Nuclear Weapons*, Brookings Press 1999.

77439810R00135

Made in the USA
Middletown, DE
21 June 2018